Mackinac Connection:

An Insider's Guide

Amy McVeigh

Mackinac Publishing,
Mackinac Island, Michigan

10 9 8 7 6 5 4 3 2

Library of Congress Cataloging-in-Publication Data

McVeigh, Amy,
    Mackinac Connection: An Insider's Guide/Amy McVeigh
        p.   cm.
    Bibliography   Includes index.
        1. Mackinac Island (Mich. :Island)--Description and travel--Guidebooks.   2. Mackinac Island (Mich.)--Description--Guidebooks.
I. Title.
F572.M16M38   1989
917.74'923--dc20
                                                        89-12356
                                                        CIP

ISBN 0-9623213-0-3

Cover artwork by Martha Dunham. Copyright, The Gallery, 1987. Reprinted with permission. Cover artwork is based on a poster available at The Gallery on Mackinac Island.

When it went to press, the information in Mackinac Connection: An Insider's Guide was complete and verified through independent research and contact with businesses. Information is based on 1989 prices and businesses.

If you love this book and want to order copies for all of your friends (which is strongly encouraged), please see page 168.

Dedicated to:

my parents, Hugh and Kathryn McVeigh, who gave me a childhood filled with the enchantment of Mackinac Island summers...

and to

my husband, Jeff Braun, who has been extraordinarily supportive of this project and whose companionship makes me look forward to many years of happiness on and off Mackinac Island...

and to

my daughter, Shawn McVeigh-Braun, who will never know the wonder of a Mackinac Island summer, but whose brief life taught her parents the importance of enjoying the beautiful people and beautiful places in our lives.

ACKNOWLEDGEMENTS

A book like this requires lots of input. I'd bore you naming everyone involved, but some deserve special credit:

All the Mackinac Island business people, summer workers, summer residents, and year-round residents who put up with my constant questioning. Sara Bolger from the Mackinac Island Chamber of Commerce, who understood the hurdles and provided information and support with a smile. David Armour, Phil Porter, and Keith Widder from the Mackinac Island State Park Commission who opened their arms and their archives.

Margaret Doud, Wes Maurer, Sr., Melinda Porter, Bill Rabe, and Harry Ryba for their insights. Hugh McVeigh for his editorial contributions and marketing know-how. Kathy McVeigh for her content contributions, particularly in the first and seventh chapters.

Drieka DeGraff for Herculean editorial input, map development, and marketing ideas. Kathleen Searing whose artistic talents grace the external and internal design. Wes Maurer, Jr., for advice and introduction to Ed Klimczak, the printer from Model Printing Services in Alpena.

Colleen Robar, whose promotional prowess is immense. Tom Hitchman, for without his Macintosh computer, the price would have soared. Jim Cubbin, Mary Cunningham, and Kathy Hunt for their editorial skills. Jack Keaton and Sue Farrar for verifying the hiking and biking routes in the rain. Dave McVeigh for his last-minute fact-checking skills. All the rest of my family and friends for constant marketing and editorial advice and encouragement.

Jeff Braun for everything -- photography, editing, encouragement, marketing, and most of all, humor. If I forgot anyone, let me know; I'll buy you a pound of fudge!

TABLE OF CONTENTS

Just in case you aren't sold on a Mackinac trip yet, usual and unusual reasons are outlined here.

Each season has its own feel on Mackinac Island. This chapter will help you figure out the best time to visit.

There are lots of ways to get here. You can drive to Mackinaw City or St. Ignace and take a ferry, take a commercial flight to the island's airport, or power in yourself -- by boat or plane.

Stay for more than the day if you can. From inexpensive bed and breakfasts to ritzy hotels, there's room for you.

Getting around on Mackinac Island is a special treat. Walk, ride a bike, or ride in a surrey with the fringe on top!

Most people can't live on fudge alone, so more than 40 restaurants take care of visitors' and residents' appetites. Learn their specialities and idiosyncrasies so you can pick the spots you'll most enjoy. We'll also explore the island after the sun sets behind the Mackinac Bridge.

The island's shopping scene is as varied as the island's visitors. Get the scoop on all the shops.

Mackinac Island's natural attractions are legendary. Some of them are hard to miss, and for some it helps to have an expert to guide your explorations. We'll go on a tour together.

This is history for the traveler, not the historian. You'll learn all the key dates and characters -- and there's no quiz at the end! We'll go on three tours together.

Sporting enthusiasts love Mackinac's clean air and varied terrain. The secrets are here, including the cheapest tennis courts, best place to find stones for skipping, and best routes for biking and hiking.

This is the insider's chapter of the insider's book. How to enjoy romance and weddings on the island, how to stay longer, and how to plan a convention. We'll also explore ways to get involved, stay in touch, and take a piece of the island home.

From A (Addresses) to W (weather) here are important, amusing, and esoteric things that natives know about Mackinac. (I couldn't come up with an X-Y-Z.)

FEATURES

THOUGHTS FROM OTHER ISLAND INSIDERS

MAPS

LIST OF PHOTOGRAPHS
AND PHOTO CREDITS

Photo credits:

Jeff Braun: 7, 12, 20, 26, 35, 42, 45, 53, 56, 64, 75, 80, 88, 128, 138, 148, 151, 152, 158

Grand Hotel: 23

Mackinac Island State
Park Commission: 97, 101, 104, 107, 109, 112, 119, 121, 140

Michigan Travel Bureau: 5, 48, 129, 144, 155

Mission Point Resort: 32

1
WHY COME TO
MACKINAC ISLAND?

"Mackinac, as a health resort, is unsurpassed. Its cool air and pure water, together with its natural beauties and historic association, are just what are needed to bring back the glow of health to the faded cheek, and send the warm currents of life dancing through the system with youthful vigor. In Mackinac, you eat with a new relish, and sleep as when a child. You row, you ramble like boys and girls, scarcely able to keep your buoyancy within bounds. You need to set a double guard upon your dignity, lest it escape you entirely."

1879 travel brochure

Mackinac is a timeless place. The peacefulness that goes with living in a horse-drawn world is evident immediately. Patient horses with fancy rigs are tied up outside the post office. Because there are no mailing addresses, all residents pick up the mail at the post office. Here gossip is exchanged, and notices of meetings are posted on the bulletin board. A clock on one cottage wall reads beneath the hands, "Who Cares?" No one, that's who.

Mackinac is a humorous place. The beginning of the tourist season is marked each spring by a ceremony in which the pool table is taken out of the only year-round tavern to make room for tourists. One of the most successful business owners rides a bicycle around with a cash box in the basket. There's a dog listed in the phone book. The daily "noon" fire siren goes off about five minutes late.

Mackinac is a beautiful place. As the promotional brochures say, Mackinac Island is a jewel in the sparkling waters of Lake Huron. Its majestic tree covered cliffs contrast with an endless blue sky. The air is clean and the woods are overflowing with wild flowers. Nature lovers, sporting enthusiasts, and romantics all revel in the beauty.

Mackinac is a gentle place. People smile and say hello, whether they know you or not. This is a caring community. When the lighthouse across the water on Round Island was crumbling, Mackinac lead the drive to save it. In the 1960's, when other parks had conflicts with people congregating and disturbing the peace at night, Mackinac installed an automatic sprinkler system to dampen the problem in its main park.

Tnere are a few things that Mackinac is not. It is not Palm Springs, where there are multitudes of high-brow shops. It is not New York City, where nightlife is the life and gourmet restaurants abound. And it is not new. It is old and comfortable, like a favorite pair of jeans. Just the way we like it.

Let's go ramble, boys and girls!

2
WHEN TO COME
TO MACKINAC ISLAND

Mackinac Island's tourist season used to be short:
Independence Day to Labor Day. But that has changed, and
many visitors are discovering the wonder of a spring, fall,
or winter trip to the island. The majority of visitors still
come to the island between mid-June and mid-September,
but most hotels are open from mid-May until mid-October.
And a few are open year-round.

When planning your trip, consider what you want out of
your Mackinac vacation, what the weather is likely to be,
and what events the island has scheduled.

If I had to characterize the seasons on Mackinac, I'd say
spring is best for nature lovers, with trillium carpeting
the woods and lilacs in bloom downtown. Summer is for
the tourist; the history is re-enacted daily, all the shops,
restaurants, and attractions are open, the weather is
gorgeous, and the streets are hopping. Fall is for island
aficionados. The trails are beautiful when the trees
change colors, many of the stores and restaurants are still
open, and the pace changes dramatically as the tourist

season winds down. Winter is for adventurers and athletes. Getting to the island in the winter is an adventure in itself, and staying here is a wonderful athletic endeavor, with great cross-country skiing and winter hiking.

WEATHER

Because of the island's location in the Straits of Mackinac, the weather can change rapidly. Daytime summer temperatures are at least 10 degrees cooler than summers in Detroit or Chicago, but with the breezes from the lake, the temperatures seem even cooler. Summer nights on Mackinac are a pleasant relief from the heat on the mainland. Bring a jacket or a warm sweater and a raincoat, just in case!

Average temperatures are as follows:

May	June	July	Aug	Sept	Oct
62/44	70/52	77/58	74/58	66/51	52/38

(High/Low)

ANNUAL EVENTS

The Straits area (which includes Mackinac Island, Mackinaw City, and St. Ignace) has a continuous calendar of interesting annual events. The dates vary by year, so please check with the chambers of commerce (see page 147). You may want to plan your trip to take advantage of one or more of these (1989 dates):

May Events

Mackinaw City Pageant. On Memorial Day weekend, Mackinaw City re-enacts life at Fort Michilimackinac between 1715 and 1781.

June Events

Mackinac Island Lilac Festival. During the second week of June, Mackinac Island has a week-long celebration of the blooming of the island's beautiful lilacs. This is the island's equivalent of a small town summer festival, complete with a parade, a lilac queen, and lots of events for children and adults.

Mackinac Island Chamber Music Festival. During the third and fourth week in June, the island attracts many well-known chamber musicians to perform at various locations.

Straits Area Antique Auto Show. On the last weekend in June, St. Ignace plays host to a huge antique auto show.

**Many of the island's lilac trees
are over 200 years old.**

July Events

Independence Day. Mackinac Island, Mackinaw City, and St. Ignace all have celebrations and fireworks. The island's old-fashioned Fourth of July includes a stone skipping contest, sack races, and a greased-pole climbing competition.

Chicago-to-Mackinac Yacht Race. After departing Chicago the third Saturday in July, the yachts arrive on the island about three days later. The island swings into high gear as 300 sailboats and their crews arrive on the island to celebrate the end of their race.

Port Huron-to-Mackinac Yacht Race. After departing Port Huron the fourth Saturday in July, the yachts arrive on the island about three days later. The celebration is even larger this week, as many of the crews celebrate the end of both races.

Christmas in July. On July 25, Mackinac Island celebrates Christmas with a Christmas bazaar.

August Events

Horse Show and Bicycle Races. The first weekend in August is a big one for the island's year-round and summer residents. The horse show, held at Great Turtle Park, is an opportunity to show off equestrian skills. The bicycle races feature relay teams and individual cyclists racing around the island's perimeter, capped off by a jump in the Straits by the winning team.

Antique Boat Show. During the second weekend in August, the Les Cheneaux Islands in Michigan's upper peninsula play host to a large antique boat show. The Arnold Line runs a special ferry from Mackinac Island to Hessel, where the show is held.

Mountain Bike Race. On the third weekend in August, cyclists race on mountain bikes through Mackinac Island's interior.

September Events

Bridge Walk   On Labor Day, Michigan's Governor leads an early morning walk over the Mackinac Bridge.

Mackinac Island Road Race.   During the second weekend of September, the island hosts a foot race around its perimeter.

❝ *My favorite way to spend a day on Mackinac is cross-country skiing after a 24-hour snow storm when the trees are weighed down with a foot of snow and there is no sign of any other humans... My advice for the first time visitor: 1) bring comfortable walking shoes and clothing; and 2) be patient, part of the beauty of Mackinac is the pace.* ❞

Melinda Porter, long-time island resident

**Spring is a wonderful time
to explore the island's beauty.**

3
GETTING HERE

Summer visitors to Mackinac Island arrive in one of three ways: 1) ferry after arriving in Mackinaw City or St. Ignace; 2) private or commercial plane; or 3) private boat.

DRIVING

The majority of island visitors drive to the closest point on the mainland, (Mackinaw City from the south or St. Ignace from the north) and then take a ferry across the Straits to Mackinac Island. If you haven't been over the Mackinac Bridge, I'd recommend you do just the opposite: coming from the south, go over the bridge, and take the ferry from St. Ignace; coming from the north, go over the bridge and take the ferry from Mackinaw City. The bridge, which connects Michigan's upper and lower peninsulas, is impressive and the view is fabulous. The charge is $1.50 per car each way, and it only takes an extra ten minutes. Whichever city you depart from, you won't have any problem finding the boat docks; they are well marked.

Mackinaw City is 280 miles from Detroit, 390 from Chicago, 430 from Cleveland, 225 from Lansing, 360 from Milwaukee, 40 from Petoskey, and 100 from Traverse City. St. Ignace is 55 miles from Sault Ste. Marie and 7 miles from Mackinaw City.

If you are coming from the south and have the time, consider the scenic routes U.S. 23 around Michigan's eastern shore or U.S. 31 around its western shore. If you take I-75 northbound, look for some of my favorite milestones: the sign that says "Tourist and Elk Herd Information, Exit 310," Sea Shell City (exit 326), and the first view of the Mackinac Bridge (mile marker 334). Mackinaw City is exit 337 northbound and St. Ignace is exit 344A northbound. If you are coming from the north, St. Ignace is exit 344 and Mackinaw City is exit 338. The

route to the boat docks is well marked in both Mackinaw City and St. Ignace.

If you will be visiting other areas in Michigan after your stay on Mackinac Island, you may want to stop in the State of Michigan buildings on either side of the bridge. The people there have a wealth of information about other Michigan attractions.

FERRY

There are three ferry companies operating between Mackinac Island and the mainland: Arnold Transit, Shepler's, and Star Line. All of them operate from both cities. The rates are standardized at $9.00 round trip for adults and $5.25 for children (ages 5 - 12). Bicycles can be taken across for $3.00, and there is no extra charge for luggage. Ferries run regular schedules from Mackinaw City from mid-May through October, and from St. Ignace from mid-May through late December.

During the summer season (mid-June through Labor Day), boats run about every half hour from 8:00 a.m. to 7:00 p.m. daily. There is also a late-night service available, but because the schedule is variable, you should check with the boat companies. Boats are less frequent during the spring and fall, so you may want to call the ferry companies or the Mackinac Island Chamber of Commerce (see page 147) and get a current schedule. You can purchase your ticket on the boat dock or at one of the kiosks (you can't miss them) between the expressway and the boat dock.

If you read the billboards along I-75, you'll realize how competitive the ferry business is. Everyone has the fastest, safest, largest, or "bestest" boats. You can't go wrong with any of the companies. Here are a few things you may want to consider when choosing a ferry:

Arnold Transit (906/847-3351) - Arnold Transit's catamarans are the newest boats on the Straits and, for the record, are the fastest, making the Mackinaw City crossing in 14 minutes and the St. Ignace crossing in 9 minutes. For a more leisurely ride to the island, Arnold has boats that take about 40 minutes to make the Mackinaw City run and 30 minutes for the St. Ignace run.

Arnold has two docks in Mackinaw City. The "cats" depart from the Arnold dock. (The other dock is called the State dock.) Day parking is free, and overnight parking is $1.00 per day. Secured outside parking or inside parking is available for an additional charge. Valet parking is available for $3.00. Arnold is also the only company to continue operations past October. Arnold's dock on Mackinac Island is in the middle of town.

Shepler's (616/436-5023) - Shepler's boats are all fast, and Shepler advertises an 18-minute trip and a "hydro-plane" ride. Shepler's has one dock in each city. It has a super-efficient parking and loading system, and offers secured parking for those who are interested. Parking is free for the day or overnight (for one or two nights), and $2.50 per night for additional nights. Secured or inside parking is also available. Valet parking is available for $2.50. Shepler's Car Care Service will wash your car and perform light maintenance while you are on the island. Shepler's dock on the island is on the western end of town.

Star Line (906/643-7635) - Star Line is the newest and smallest of the ferry companies, offering an 18-minute ride. It has one dock in Mackinaw City and two docks (Main and Railroad) in St. Ignace. Day parking is free and overnight parking is $2.00. The Star Line Dock on the island is on the western end of town, just west of the Shepler dock.

Whichever ferry company you choose, make sure to see that your luggage gets on the boat on the way to the island. When you reach the island, you'll need to identify it on the dock and arrange for transportation to your hotel or bed and breakfast. All of the hotels have porters who meet the boats and assist with luggage. They carry it in bicycles with huge baskets. A tip of $1 per bag is customary. On the return trip, you must claim your luggage from your hotel porter on the dock before it will be put on the boat.

Dock porters ride bikes with specially reinforced baskets.

PLANE

Mackinac Island has an airport with a 3,500 foot paved, lighted runway that gets a lot of use in the summer. The landing fee is $5 for a single engine plane and $10 for a multi-engine plane, and there is plenty of parking space ($5 single, $10 multi-engine). Be sure to plan ahead, though, because the airport does not sell fuel. Night lights can be activated on a UNICOM frequency. For more information, call the Mackinac Island Airport at 906/847-3231.

Northwest Airlines (800/225-2525) offers regularly scheduled flights from Chicago and Detroit to Emmet County Airport in Pellston, Michigan. Pellston is about 12 miles south of Mackinaw City. From there, you can take an automobile taxi service (call Wolverine Stages 616/539-8635) or an air taxi service (call Great Lakes Air 906/643-7165). Wolverine Stages charges $10 per person one way from Pellston to the Mackinaw City boat docks. Great Lakes Air charges $35 per person one way from Pellston to the Mackinac Island Airport, based on a two-person minimum.

If you think you are going to miss the last boat to Mackinac Island, call ahead for reservations and Great Lakes Air will fly you from St. Ignace to the island for $12 per person. Between late December and early May, Great Lakes Air flies a regular schedule because air travel is the only way to get to the island (except for a snowmobile if the ice bridge is formed).

PRIVATE BOAT

Mackinac Island is a favorite of Great Lakes boaters. The state-owned marina's 78 slips can accommodate up to 100 boats and are full most of the season. A few slips are permanently assigned, and the others are available on a first-come, first-served basis. When the slips are full, boaters may anchor in the harbor for free. There is a seven-day maximum stay in the marina.

Fees for overnight stays are $11.75 for boats under 21 feet long. Larger boats are charged per foot on a graduated scale from $.58/foot for up to 30 feet to $.78/foot for up to 60 feet. The fee includes water, electricity, and public rest rooms. Showers are available for $2.00 at the yacht club across the street from the marina. Don't plan your boating trip to Mackinac Island during the third or fourth weeks in July. The Chicago-to-Mackinac and Port Huron-to-Mackinac yacht races are held then, and the marina is taken over by racers.

The marina is open from mid-May to late September. Gasoline, diesel fuel, and a pump-out station are available. The harbor is 10 feet deep. If you need to make a few repairs, Mackinac Marine Supply can supply the parts (see page 92). Call the marina at 906/847-3561 for additional information.

MACKINAC ISLAND ROADS AND TRAILS

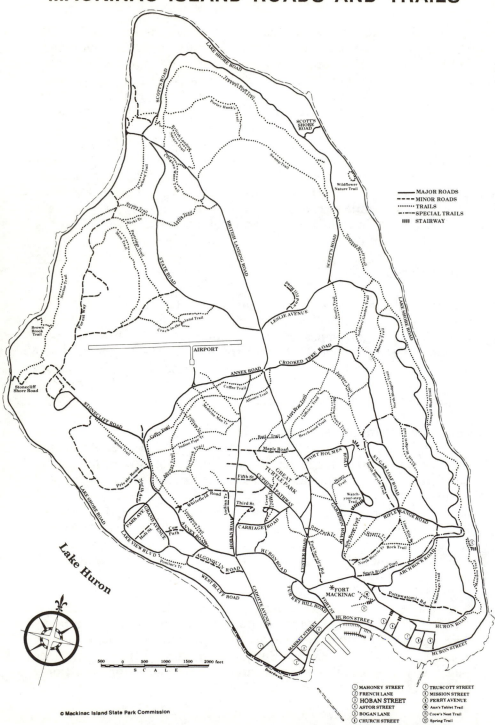

MAJOR ROADS
MINOR ROADS
TRAILS
SPECIAL TRAILS
STAIRWAY

Lake Huron

500 0 500 1000 1500 2000 feet
S C A L E

© Mackinac Island State Park Commission

① MAHONEY STREET	⑦ TRUSCOTT STREET
② FRENCH LANE	⑧ MISSION STREET
③ HOBAN STREET	⑨ FERRY AVENUE
④ ASTOR STREET	⑩ Ann's Tablet Trail
⑤ BOGAN LANE	⑪ Crow's Nest Trail
⑥ CHURCH STREET	⑫ Spring Trail

Map developed with a grant from Coastal Zone Management.
Used with permission of Mackinac State Historic Parks.

4
STAYING HERE

Mention that you are staying on Mackinac Island, and people will assume you are staying at "the hotel," referring to Mackinac's grand dame of hotels, the Grand Hotel. Many believe it is the only alternative for travelers who want to enjoy the island more than a day-long trip allows. But there is a wide variety of hotels, bed and breakfasts, and tourist homes to accommodate most budgets. There are 23 inns in all, with over 1,100 sleeping rooms.

You won't find a Sheraton or a Holiday Inn on Mackinac Island. All of the hotels are family-owned and operated and most of them are very old. With age comes charm, and some inconveniences. Most of the hotels have updated their rooms, but few have air conditioning, telephones, or televisions. If these are important to you, be sure to ask before you make a reservation. If not, enjoy the charm.

The map on the next page shows the location of most of the hotels. The list that follows the map is in alphabetical order and includes 1989 room rates, based on two occupants during the high season (mid-June through Labor Day).

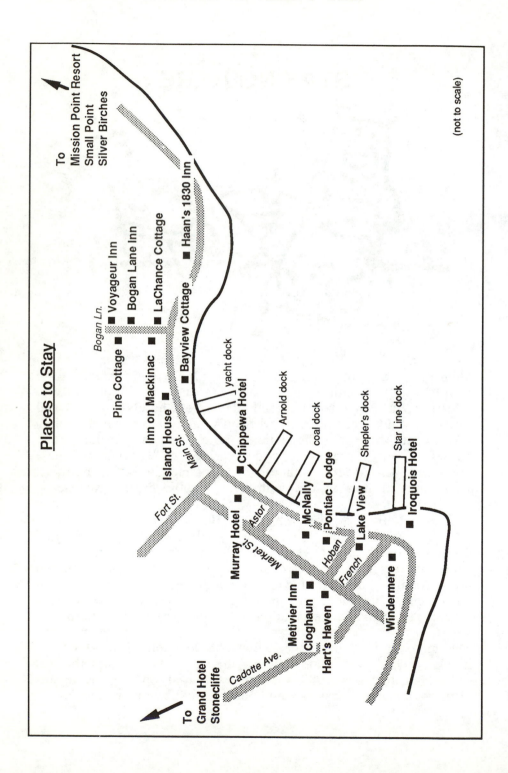

To simplify your review of accommodations, some key facts are summarized in the following:

Name	Per Room Double Rate	Meals Included	No. of Rooms
Bayview Cottage	$ 40 - 60	--	7
Bogan Lane Inn	$ 45	CB	4
Chippewa Hotel	$ 60 - 155	--	75
Cloghaun	$ 40 - 50	CB	7
Grand Hotel	$240 - 450	B, D	312
Haan's 1830 Inn	$ 60 - 175	CB	7
Hart's Haven	$ 50	CB	5
Iroquois Hotel	$ 98 - 250	--	47
Inn on Mackinac	$ 69 - 150	CB	44
Island House	$110 - 115	--	94
LaChance Cottage	$ 45 - 60	--	18
Lake View Hotel	$130 - 170	--	85
McNally Cottage	$ 30 - 55	--	8
Metivier Inn	$110 - 130	CB	17
Mission Point	$110 - 400	B	245
Murray Hotel	$ 59 - 150	--	69
Pine Cottage	$ 44 - 64	CB	18
Pontiac Lodge*	$ 95 - 140	--	9
Silver Birches*	$600 - 800/week	--	2+
Small Point	$ 45	CB	6
Stonecliffe*	$ 99 - 239	--	14+
Voyageur Inn*	$105 - 160	--	3+
Windermere	$135	CB	26

CB = Continental Breakfast
 B = Breakfast
 D = Dinner

* These places have condominiums, houses, or apartments available on a weekly basis.

Children are welcome at any of the hotels, but none allow pets.   If the hotel has a ban on smoking or has non-smoking rooms, it is indicated below.

In the high season, many of the hotels will be sold out, so it is best to call or write in advance.   For more information, contact the hotels directly.   In the off-season, you can still write to their island addresses and they will receive your letter.   Most of the hotels frequently have special packages available and off-season rates can be considerably lower than those listed.

Another economical alternative is to stay in Mackinaw City or St. Ignace, although you won't be able to enjoy the island at night if you go that route.   Both cities have campgrounds (camping is prohibited on the island) and a number of hotels and motels.   Call the chambers of commerce for more information:

Mackinaw City
616/436-5574
P.O. Box 856
Mackinaw City, MI   49710

St. Ignace
906/643-8717
11 S. State Street
St. Ignace, MI   49781.

BAYVIEW COTTAGE
P.O. Box 448, Mackinac Island, MI   49757
906/847-3295

On Main Street, just east of downtown.   Open late May to mid-September.

Rates are $40 - $60 per room, based on two occupants.   Tax is additional.   No credit cards, but personal checks are accepted.   Not air conditioned.

Bayview Cottage's primary asset is its location, near the water, on the east end of the marina.   It has seven rooms that share two bathrooms (one has a tub, the other a shower).   Try to get one of the two rooms with a bay window overlooking the harbor and Fort Mackinac.   The rooms do not have telephones or televisions.   Guests are welcome to use the porch and living room.   There are two restaurants adjacent to Bayview (see The Pub and The Oyster Bar in Chapter Six).

BOGAN LANE INN
P.O. Box 482, Mackinac Island, MI 49757
906/847-3439

On Bogan Lane, one long block east of downtown, and one block north of Huron Street. Open Memorial Day to mid-October, and often open year-round.

All rooms are $45, based on two people. Continental breakfast and tax are included. No credit cards, but personal checks are accepted. Not air conditioned. No smoking in the rooms.

After the Martin family raised their children on Mackinac Island, they decided to turn their family home into a bed and breakfast so they could share it with others. The home was built in the 1850's and has four bedrooms to rent.

The Martin's call the furniture in Bogan Lane "island furniture" rather than antique, but much of it has been in the home for years. The rooms have a warm, homey appearance and share two modern baths with tub/shower combinations. One room has one double bed, one has a double and a twin, and two have twin beds. The back bedroom (twin/twin) has a charming adjoining sun porch that has two twin beds and is ideal for children. None of the rooms has a television or telephone.

Guests are welcome to use the living room and fireplace, as well as the enclosed yard.

CHIPPEWA HOTEL
P.O. Box 250, Mackinac Island, MI 49757
906/847-3341

On Main Street at Fort Street. Open mid-May to mid-October.

Rates are $60 - $155 per room, plus tax. American Express, Visa, Master Card , and personal checks are accepted. Not air conditioned.

The Chippewa Hotel ("Chip") has been catering to the island visitor since the turn of the century. Because of its waterfront location, it is a favorite for boaters. Its heated outdoor pool and downtown location also make it popular with families.

The Chip has 75 rooms unspoiled by the modern conveniences of televisions and telephones. Most of the bathrooms have showers only. Most of the rooms on the second and third floors have been recently updated. Be sure to ask for a lake view.

The Chippewa has an excellent restaurant and a popular night spot (see Chapter Six). Its lobby is a great location to watch Main Street. It also has a function room, with a view of the harbor, that can accommodate up to 70 people.

Haan's 1830 Inn is the oldest building used as an inn.

CLOGHAUN
P.O. Box 203, Mackinac Island, MI   49757
906/847-3885

One block north of town on Market Street.   Open Memorial Day to mid-September.

Rates are $40 - 50 per room (plus tax), including continental breakfast.   Not air conditioned.

Cloghaun (pronounced Clo-han) is Gaelic for "land of little stones."   It is owned by descendents of the Donnelly family, who left Ireland during the potato famine and built the home in 1884.

The colonial-style inn has seven bedrooms, two of which have private baths with tubs.   All the rooms connect and can be rented as suites.   Each room has its own sink.

The guests may use a small parlor with a fireplace and piles of books for rainy days.

GRAND HOTEL
Mackinac Island, MI   49757
906/847-3331

On a hill about 1/2 mile northwest of downtown.   Open mid-May to early November.

Rates including breakfast and dinner are $240 - $450 per room.   There are no off-season discounts.   Because tipping is not allowed, an 18% surcharge is added to the above rates, and the 4% Michigan tax is applied after the surcharge.   A $3.50/person charge is added for round-trip luggage transportation.   Visa, Master Card,and personal checks are accepted.   Four rooms are air conditioned. Room service available.

People call it "the hotel" on the island, Hollywood producers choose it as the site for romantic movies, and honeymooners, dignitaries and conventioneers trip over one another to stay there.   It is the Grand Hotel, the world's largest summer hotel, built in 1887 and featuring a 660-foot veranda overlooking the Straits of Mackinac.

The Grand was built by a consortium of railroad and steamship companies seeking to increase vacation travel to northern Michigan.   Its success sparked the development of many of the large Victorian homes on the island.   A gamble at the time, the Grand is now a consistent success story; occupancy rates reportedly run in the 90% range. The Grand has the capacity to handle groups of up to 1,000 people, so the convention business is big business at the Grand.

Each of the 312 rooms is decorated differently, most in the style of noted designer Carleton Varney (who decorated the Greenbrier Resort in West Virginia).   The Grand has just completed a 10-year renovation plan; Varney designed much of the furniture and fabrics exclusively for the hotel.   The rooms have private baths (tub/shower combinations) and telephones.   They do not have televisions.

When guests tire of relaxing on the veranda, they may enjoy swimming in the serpentine pool, wandering through the gardens, golfing at the nine-hole golf course, playing tennis on one of the four clay courts, working out on the hotel's exercise course, playing shuffleboard, or dancing in the Terrace Room.

The Grand has eight restaurants and lounges, ranging from the formality of the Main Dining Room and multi-course meals to the relaxation of a hamburger and lemonade at the Pool Grill   (see Chapter Six).

Most guests wear informal resort clothing during the day, but after six men are required to wear coats and ties, and dresses and suits are "preferred" for women.

The Grand Hotel (opposite), is the island's largest hotel, with 312 rooms.

HAAN'S 1830 INN
P.O. Box 123, Mackinac Island, MI 49757
906/847-6244

Four blocks east of downtown on Huron Street. Open late May through mid-October.

Rates per room including continental breakfast are $60 - $175, plus tax. No credit cards, but personal checks are accepted. Not air conditioned.

As the name implies, the main building of this inn was built in 1830. It was later the residence of Colonel Preston, one of the last officers at Fort Mackinac and mayor of the island at the turn of the century. With the 1847 addition, the inn has seven bedrooms, each beautifully decorated and furnished with period antiques and named after a famous island figure.

Each of the four rooms in the addition (three doubles and one twin/twin) has a private bath with shower or tub and shower. In the main house, two rooms (one double/double and one twin/twin) share a large bath with antique tub and shower. The Colonel William Preston Suite in the main house has a bed-sitting room, equipped kitchen, and private bath with tub and shower. It sleeps four.

Continental breakfast is served daily in the dining room, and guests are welcome to enjoy the inn's three porches and the front parlors.

HART'S HAVEN
P.O. Box 266, Mackinac Island, MI 49757
906/847-3854

On Market Street, at French Lane. Open late May to late September.

Rates are $50 per room (without tax) for two people, including a continental breakfast. No credit cards, but personal checks are accepted. Not air conditioned.

The Hart's Haven brochure describes its rooms as "motel-like" and that is an accurate description. The four rooms are small and the furnishings are functional. Each room has its own bathroom with a shower. There are no telephones or televisions. There is also an efficiency apartment available on a weekly basis.

IROQUOIS HOTEL
Mackinac Island, MI 49757
906/847 - 3321

On Main Street, at the west end of downtown. Open mid-May to late October.

Rates are $98 - $230 per room, plus tax and a $1.50 per person hotel baggage charge. Master Card, Visa, and personal checks are accepted. Not air conditioned.

Perched on the water's edge, the Iroquois rooms lay claim to the best view of the harbor, the Straits, and the Mackinac Bridge. The decor is stunning -- "island resort" at its best. Each of the 47 rooms is decorated differently, with a collection of wicker and wood. Each room has its own bath, with a tub/shower combination. Some rooms have balconies. The rooms do not have telephones. Rental televisions are available.

Guests may enjoy the sunny three-room lobby overlooking Main Street and the Straits, the front porch overlooking Main Street, and the back terrace near the shore. Room service continental breakfast is available at an additional charge. The Iroquois also has an excellent restaurant, which serves lunch and dinner (see Carriage House, in Chapter Six).

The Iroquois Hotel was transformed from a rectangular box into a building with interesting peaks, turrets, and porches.

INN ON MACKINAC
P.O. Box 476, Mackinac Island, MI   49757
906/847-3361

On the corner of Main Street and Bogan Lane, one long block east of downtown.   Open mid-May to late October.

Rates are $69 - $150 (without tax) per room including a continental breakfast.   Visa, Master Card, and personal checks are accepted.   Air conditioned.

The Inn on Mackinac is the island's newest entry on the bed and breakfast scene.   Like many of the larger, older homes, it served as employee housing for years before becoming a tourist home (Chateau Beaumont) and annex to the Murray Hotel.   In 1988 it was the talk of the town as it blossomed into 12 colors, a bit unusual on this island.   Then the facility was expanded and renovated, doubling the number of rooms to 44.

Each of the rooms is furnished with antiques and has a television and individual air conditioning (deemed necessary after the heat wave of 1988). Rooms have private baths, most with tub/shower combinations. Guests can enjoy the wraparound porch, patio, and parlor with fireplace. Some rooms have balconies.

ISLAND HOUSE
Mackinac Island, MI   49757
906/847-3347

On Main Street, just east of downtown.   Open mid-May through mid-October.

Rates are $110 - $115 per room, plus tax.   Visa, Master Card, and personal checks are accepted.   Air conditioning on the fourth floor only.

The Island House is the oldest hotel on the island, originally built in 1852. It has been expanded several times since then, and is registered as a Michigan historic site.

Almost all of the Island House's 94 rooms were upgraded in the late 1980's. All of the rooms have private baths with tub/shower combinations. The rooms do not have telephones or televisions. Ask for a room with a lake view, and if you like cozy rooms with dormers, try the fourth floor. For spacious two-room suites, try rooms 224 or 324.

There is a two-room Victorian style lobby with a television for guests to use, but most spend their time on the huge porch (the island's second largest) overlooking the marina. The Guvner's Table serves up breakfast and dinner and The Guvner's Lounge usually has evening entertainment (see Chapter Six). If you are planning a meeting, the Conference Room can accommodate up to 50 people.

LACHANCE COTTAGE
P.O. Box 55, Mackinac Island, MI   49757
906/847-3526

On Main Street at Bogan Lane, one long block east of downtown. Open late May through late September.

Rates are $45 - 60 per room, based on two occupants. Tax is additional. No credit cards, but personal checks are accepted. Not air conditioned.

Built as a private home before the turn of the century, LaChance now rents its 18 rooms to the public. They are functional and clean. All share full baths; there are two baths on each of the home's three floors. There are no televisions or telephones. Some of the rooms have sinks.

LAKE VIEW HOTEL
P.O. Box 160, Mackinac Island, MI   49757
906/847-3384

On Main Street, between Hoban Avenue and French Lane. Open mid-May through mid-October.

Rates are $130 - $170 per room, based on two occupants. Tax is additional. American Express, Visa, Master Card and personal checks are accepted. About half the rooms are air conditioned. Room service available.

The Lake View Hotel owns the category of the newest old hotel on Mackinac Island. Originally built in 1858, the Lake View was extensively rebuilt in the late 1980's.

Its 85 rooms are decorated with cherrywood furnishings and floral wallpaper and fabric. Each room has a private bath (tub/shower combination) and telephone. Televisions are not available. Some of the rooms have whirlpools. The most popular rooms are the tower rooms, with their unique shapes and pleasant views.

The Lake View has the island's only enclosed, heated swimming pool. Its meeting rooms wrap around the pool, and can accommodate up to 350 people. Beverages are available pool side, and meal service is available at three hotel restaurants (see James Cable Dining Room, Pilot House, and Hoban Street Cafe in Chapter Six).

McNALLY COTTAGE
P.O. Box 366, Mackinac Island, MI 49757
906/847-3565 - summer
313/241-7454 - winter

On Main Street, between Astor and Hoban Streets. Open late May through mid-September.

Rates are $30 - 55 per room, based on two occupants. Tax is additional. No credit cards, but personal checks are accepted. Not air conditioned. Smoking is not allowed in the rooms.

McNally Cottage celebrated its 100th year of welcoming guests to Mackinac Island in 1989. It was built by Michael McNally in 1889, and is still owned and operated by his relatives.

The eight rooms are simple, clean, and homey. Half the rooms have private baths and half share a bath. The rooms do not have telephones or televisions. Ask for "Rosebud" or, if you have children with you, ask for the suite.

Guests can watch the Main Street activity from the charming blue-and-white enclosed front porch.

METIVIER INN
P.O. Box 285, Mackinac Island, MI 49757
906/847-6234

On Market Street, and between Astor and Hoban Streets. Open mid-May through mid-October.

Rates are $110 - $130 (without tax) per room per night, based on double occupancy. Rates include continental breakfast. Master Card, Visa, and personal checks are accepted. Not air conditioned.

Metivier is a charming Victorian-style inn, with 15 rooms and two efficiency apartments. Most of the inn was built in 1984 but, with its architecture and location on historic Market Street, it has the aura of a much older establishment.

The rooms are beautifully decorated, mostly with new wicker and brass furnishings. Two rooms have antique furniture. For a special occasion, ask for one of the two turret rooms. Each room has a queen bed and a private bath; all have tub/shower combinations except those on the third floor, which have showers only. The rooms do not have televisions or telephones.

Guests are free to enjoy the large front porch and watch the parade of people, horses and bicycles go by on Market Street.

Winter Wonderland

"The words I would use about winter are 'quiet' and 'peaceful.' We get our home back. I don't mean that as a slur on the tourists, because come spring we are ready for everyone to come back and for all the activity to begin again. I guess you'd say I can't wait for it (the summer season) to end and can't wait for it to begin." Jesse Doud, owner of Jesse's Chuck Wagon, echoed many year-round residents' sentiments when she made that statement to the island newspaper, the *Town Crier*.

There are about 600 people who make Mackinac Island their year-round home. Most of them are descendants of the early Straits area Indian and French residents. Most of the permanent homes are in Harrisonville in the center of the island, and at Stonecliffe near the airport.

From the time the last Arnold Line boat stops running in late December until the ice bridge between the island and St. Ignace freezes (usually in February, but sometimes not at all), the only way to get on or off the island is by plane.

When the ice bridge freezes, islanders mark the trail with Christmas trees, and it becomes a winter highway, with snowmobilers, skiers, and walkers making the trip frequently. The ice bridge usually thaws in late March, and boat service resumes in May.

The island children attend school at the Mackinac Island public school, which has about 90 students, kindergarten through twelfth grade. There's no bus service; they ride their bikes as long as possible, and then snowmobiles become the primary mode of transportation.

The grocery store, drug store, and Mustang Lounge are about the only commercial establishments open year round. The residents spend their time catching up with friends and family that they didn't have much time to see during the busy summer season, preparing buildings and businesses for the next season, and relaxing. Ste. Anne's Church and the Mustang Lounge become the centers of social activity.

The island's hiking trails and carriage roads make beautiful cross country ski trails. The snow is unspoiled by automobile exhaust, and because snowmobiles are restricted from many areas, the trails are left untracked. Stonecliffe, Bogan Lane Inn, Voyageur Inn, and Pontiac Lodge are all open in the winter, catering to the cross-country skiers. If you really want to know Mackinac Island, plan a trip here in the winter.

MISSION POINT RESORT
P.O. Box 430, Mackinac Island, MI 49757
906/847-3312

On Mission Point, about 3 / 4 mile east of downtown. Open mid-May to mid-October.

Room rates are $170 - $400 per room in Huron Court (includes full breakfast buffet) and $110 - $150 per room in Mission Court (includes continental breakfast). Tax is additional. Visa, Master Card, Discover, and personal *checks are accepted. Not air conditioned. Non-smoking rooms and room service available.*

After undergoing a multi-million dollar renovation, Mission Point Resort now boasts that it's "Mackinac Island's newest and most complete waterfront resort." The resort is located on 18 acres and has 245 rooms, including 92 suites. Originally built by Moral Re-Armament in the late 1950's and early 1960's, it was briefly a liberal arts college. It struggled as a hotel in collegiate clothes for two decades until its current owner purchased it with a plan to make it a premier resort. The hotel appears to be on its way, with 27 new meeting rooms, conference facilities to handle groups up to 600, and extensive renovations throughout.

**Mission Point Resort is
the island's second largest hotel.**

Rooms are available in two buildings: Huron Court and Mission Court. In Huron Court, which is connected to the hotel's main lodge, the decor is Country French with lots of pine furniture. Room rates in Huron Court include a breakfast buffet in the hotel's Point Dining Room. Mission

Court is at the west end of the complex, a bit of a trek outdoors from the main lodge, and offers an economical alternative. Room rates in Mission Court include a continental breakfast, available in Mission Court's Johnson Hall. Each room has a private bath with a tub/shower combination, a color television and a telephone.

The Main Lodge, which houses the resort's lobby, front desk, two restaurants (see Chapter Six), and several meeting rooms, is a stunning "lodge-up-north" on a grand scale. Mission Point has an outdoor swimming pool and hot tub, tennis courts, fitness center, arcade and pool tables, and bicycle rental.

MURRAY HOTEL
P.O. Box 476, Mackinac Island, MI 49757
906/847-3361

On Main Street, in the middle of downtown. Open mid-May to mid-October.

Rates are $59 - 150 per room (tax additional). Visa, Master Card, and personal checks accepted. Air conditioned.

The Murray Hotel has been offering friendly, family-style service to island visitors since 1882. It has maintained its old-world charm while updating all of its public areas and most of its rooms.

Most of the 69 rooms are decorated with antiques and have pleasant touches such as lace swags over the beds. All except the least expensive rooms have televisions, and all have air conditioning and private baths (most with tub/shower combinations). The two whirlpool suites are wonderfully luxurious. The blue and white lobby, with its piano and wicker chairs is a wonderful place to hide out on a cool day. The front porch is a prime location for downtown people-watching.

Murray's Dining Room and the Murray Deli and Cocktail Lounge are in the hotel (see Chapter Six).

PINE COTTAGE

P.O. Box 519, Mackinac Island, MI 49757
906/847-3820

Open mid-May to mid-October. On Bogan Lane, one long block east of downtown, and one block north of Main Street.

Rates are $44 for a double with a shared bath and $64 for a room that sleeps two to four with a private bath. Tax is additional. Continental breakfast is included American Express, Visa, Master Card, and personal checks accepted. Not air conditioned. Smoking is not allowed.

Pine Cottage Tourist Home appropriately bills itself as "comfortable accommodations for the budget minded guest." The decorating is plain, the furniture is functional, and the rates are low. Each of the 18 rooms has a television set, but no phone. Some of the baths are tub only and others are shower only.

Guests are free to enjoy the small living area and the large wraparound porch.

PONTIAC LODGE
P.O. Box 495, Mackinac Island, MI 49757
906/847-3364

Hoban Street just north of Main. Open year-round. Rates are $95 - $140 per room plus tax. Visa, Master Card, Discover, and personal checks are accepted. Some air conditioned rooms.

Pontiac Lodge is geared to the traveler who is planning a longer stay on the island. Its nine efficiency rooms are new, clean, and utilitarian. They have refrigerators, sinks, microwave ovens, stoves, private baths with showers, color televisions, and telephones. Coin laundry is available, and the coffee pot is always on in the morning.

On Market Street, Metivier Inn was transformed
from a house into a large bed and breakfast.

SILVER BIRCHES
P.O. Box 281, Mackinac Island, MI   49757
906/847-3238

*Three miles east of downtown on Lake Shore Drive. Open
May 1 - October 1.*

Two houses are available and they rent for $600 - $800 per week, depending on house size and number of guests. Occasionally, the proprietors will rent rooms by the night if available.   No credit cards, but personal checks are accepted.   Not air conditioned.

Silver Birches offers an unusual alternative for families or friends who want to spend an economical week or more on the island.   Silver Birches rents two homes that can each accommodate two to eight people comfortably.

The houses were built at the turn of the century and share a large lot with a log home that the proprietors occupy. The rental homes are rustic and decorated with functional furniture.   Each has one full bath, equipped kitchen, living/dining areas, television, and telephone.

The homes have a beautiful view of the lake and the property's private beach.

SMALL POINT
P.O. Box 427, Mackinac Island, MI   49757
906/847-3758

About 3 / 4 of a mile east of downtown on Lake Shore Drive. Open June 1 - Labor Day.

Rates are $45 per room, based on two occupants. Continental breakfast and use of a bicycle is included, but tax is additional.   No credit cards, but personal checks are accepted.   Not air conditioned.   Non-smoking rooms available.

Small Point is a pleasant alternative away from the downtown scene, located east of town near the water.   It was built in 1882 as a private summer house and has six rooms available.

All but one of the rooms share a bath.   The rooms do not have televisions or telephones.   Guests are free to join the owners, John and Lois Findley, in the living room or on the front porch for conversation.

STONECLIFFE
P.O. Box 338, Mackinac Island, MI   49757
906/847-3355

On the western bluff of the island, approximately 2 miles from downtown.   Open mid-May through the end of October, and Christmas and New Year's.

Rates are $99 - $239 per room or condominium, based on double occupancy, plus tax.   Visa, Master Card, Discover, and personal checks accepted.   Not air conditioned.   Non-smoking rooms are available.

If your Mackinac vacation is designed to be a "get-away-from-it-all," Stonecliffe may be the perfect hotel for you. Located on 175 acres high on the west bluff of the island, Stonecliffe is a retreat from the hustle of downtown Mackinac Island.   The English Tudor mansion was built in 1904 as a summer home for the Michael Cudahy family of Chicago, and was converted into a hotel in 1977.

The mansion has 14 rooms, all with private baths (some tub/shower combinations, others tub only).   Most are nicely decorated with period antiques.   Generally, the rooms on the second floor are larger and nicer.   Audubon A is my favorite, with a wonderful bridge view.   On the third floor, Candlelight A is a real bargain.   The rooms in the mansion do not have televisions or telephones.

Stonecliffe also offers a variety of accommodations in its newly constructed condominiums (designed in keeping with the mansion's Tudor style).   The condominiums are located right on the bluff, and most have spectacular views.   A range of accommodations is available, from private bedrooms to bi-level, two-bedroom suites with kitchens, fireplaces, patios, and solariums.   The condominiums have telephones, but no televisions.   Call Stonecliffe (906/847-3355) or Island Condo Rental (906/847-3260) to reserve a condominium.

All Stonecliffe guests are welcome to use the living room, dining room, library and back porch of the mansion.   A swimming pool and tennis courts are available and the grounds are wonderful for brisk hikes or relaxing strolls. Look for a golf course in 1990.   Meals are available either in the mansion's carriage house or at the pond house by the swimming pool   (see Chapter Six).

Transportation to and from town can be a challenge, depending on your athletic ability and sense of humor. The hotel runs a horse-drawn shuttle (free to guests, but depending on availability).   Commercial taxis are available (charge per person one way - $5) and Stonecliffe rents bicycles.   It is also a very pleasant walk (but a bit strenuous going uphill from town to the hotel).

VOYAGEUR INN
P.O. Box 520, Mackinac Island, MI   49757
906/847-6175

At the end of Bogan Lane, two blocks from downtown. Open all year.

Rates for the condominiums, which can accommodate four to six people, are $105 - $160 per night, or $500 - 800 per week, plus tax.   There is a two-night minimum stay.   No credit cards, but personal checks are accepted.   Not air conditioned.

For a week-long stay on Mackinac Island, the Voyageur Inn is an excellent option.   Its three newly constructed condominiums each have an equipped kitchen, living room, bedroom, bathroom and washer and dryer.   The condos are spacious and the decor is simple.   There are no telephones, but there are televisions.   My favorite is the bi-level with the private patio facing the woods.

WINDERMERE HOTEL
P.O. Box 538, Mackinac Island, MI   49757
906/847-3301

On Main Street, at the west end of downtown. Open mid-May to mid-October.

Rates are $135 per room, plus tax. Continental breakfast is included. Visa, Master Card and personal checks are accepted. No air conditioning.

Staying at the Windermere is staying at one of the historic summer homes on the island. The home was purchased by the Doud family around the turn of the century and has been owned and operated as an inn by generations of Douds since 1904. Margaret Doud, the inn's manager, is also the mayor of Mackinac Island.

Each of the 26 rooms is decorated differently, many with antiques and wicker. Each has its own bath. The rooms do not have televisions or telephones. Guests may enjoy a breathtaking view of the Straits from the white wicker-filled porch, or on colder days, warm up in the charming three-room lobby. Continental breakfast is served daily in the sun room. Many rooms have views of the Straits or of the Windermere's extensive garden.

5
GETTING AROUND

When you arrive at Mackinac Island for the first time, you'll be struck by what is not here: cars. Instead of the noise and smell of the horseless carriage, there is the noise and smell of the horse-drawn carriage.

Motor vehicles have been banned on the island since the turn of the century, when they were just appearing on the American scene. A group of entrepreneurs who made their living driving horse-drawn carriages and freight-hauling drays on the island were concerned that the horseless carriage would drive them out of business, so they successfully petitioned the Village Council to ban motor vehicles.

Exceptions to the ban are made for public safety (ambulance, police jeep, and fire engine) and construction vehicles (with a city-approved permit). And in the winter, island residents and visitors use snowmobiles as their primary transportation.

Without cars, your main mode of transportation while visiting the island will be your feet, a bicycle, a horse-drawn carriage, or a horse-drawn taxi.

WALKING

Walking is the easiest, least expensive, and in most weather, the best way to see most of the island. See Chapters Eight and Nine for suggested walking tours of natural and historical attractions, and Chapter Ten for walking tours designed with exercise as the priority. Wear comfortable shoes. Don't be lulled into a false sense of security because there are no cars. Look both ways before you cross the street -- bicycles, pedestrians, and horses can get in accidents too.

BICYCLING

If you are a bicycle enthusiast, take your own bike to the island. The ferry company will charge you an extra $3 per bike, but you'll have the comfort of your own bike and the freedom to use it when you want, without rental charges. Be sure to lock your bike at all times. Bicycle theft is the only recurring crime problem on the island. If you have a bicycle flag, take it off, or wrap it around the pole and secure it. The flags scare some of the horses.

Rental bicycles are available from eight rental outlets on the island. Hourly rates are reasonable ($2 an hour with a $10 deposit for a single bike). Daily rates are available. Almost all of the rental bikes are "one speed" which is fine for most of the island, as long as you don't mind pushing during the uphill climb to the island's interior. If you are feeling romantic, try a bicycle built for two! Child carriers are available, as are small bikes for children, and mini-tandems (adult on front, child on back). A limited number of three-speed and all-terrain bikes is available. On the busiest island days (yacht races, Independence Day, Labor Day), it's best to go early to rent your bike. Most rental outlets are open 8:00 a.m. - 8:00 p.m. in the high season.

Remember when you are riding that the rules of the road apply, even through there are no cars. The roads are crowded, and many people haven't ridden a bike in years. Follow these guidelines for everyone's safety:

> *Ride on the streets, not the sidewalks or boardwalk.*
> *Stay to the right.*
> *Give horses the right of way.*
> *Watch for pedestrians who have forgotten to watch for you.*
> *Do not make abrupt turns without looking around you.*
> *Do not try to read historical markers while in motion.*
> *Do not stop your bicycle in the middle of the road.*
> *Do not overload your bicycle -- with people or fudge!*

The island's terrain creates a few areas that are not safe for bicyclists. Walk your bicycle down Turkey Hill (from Huron Road between the Governor's Residence and the

**Tandem bicycles are easy to ride
as long as you don't try to steer from the back!**

Grand golf course to Fort Street) and Fort Street (from
Governor's summer residence to Main Street) and be
careful when going down the Grand Hotel Hill (Cadotte
Avenue) and Mission Hill. Bicycles are also prohibited in
the marina area, on the boat docks, and in front of the
Grand Hotel.

Park your bicycles only in designated areas downtown. Do
not leave your bicycle downtown (Main, Market and
connecting streets) between 3:00 a.m.- 7:00 a.m., or it may
be impounded. The streets are cleaned during those hours
with high-powered hoses. Bicycles that will be on the
island all summer must be licensed. Licenses are available
at the Police Station for $3. They make nice souvenirs, too.

Chapter Ten has suggested bicycle routes designed for
exercise and sightseeing, or create your own route from
the map on page 14. The following locations rent bicycles:

Iroquois Bike Rental - 847-3321 -- next to the
Shepler Dock, on the west end of town, lake side.

Island Bicycle Livery - 847-3372 -- near the Shepler
Dock, on the west end of town, lake side.

Lakeside Bikes - 847-3351 -- at the Arnold Line Dock,
in the center of town, lake side.

Mission Point Bikes - 847-3312 -- at Mission Point
Resort, east of downtown.

Orr Kids' Bikes - 847-3211 -- near the Shepler Dock,
west end of town, lake side.

Ryba's Bikes - 847-6261 -- three locations: 1) at the
Island House Hotel, just east of downtown; 2) next to
the Pancake House, on the east end of town, lake
side; and 3) near the Shepler Dock, on the west end
of town, lake side.

Street Side Bikes - 847-3351 -- on Main Street at Astor
Street, lake side, next to the Taxi Office.

CARRIAGE TOURS

A surrey with the fringe on top is a favorite for all ages, and is available in many forms on Mackinac Island. If it's your first visit to the island, you should take a carriage tour. It provides a good introduction to the island, exposing you to many sights that you can later explore in more detail.

Private Chauffeured Carriage

Private chauffeured carriages are available by the hour from Main Street in front of Marquette Park. Rates are about $8 per person, based on a minimum of four people and a maximum of seven. Stop by and make arrangements, or call Arrowhead Carriages on 847-6112, Carriage Tours on 847-6152, or Gough on 847-3391.

Many of the guides are long-time island residents, happy to answer all your questions in addition to giving you a guided tour. Tell them what you'd like to see, and they'll design a tour for you. My favorite route is to go in front of the Grand Hotel, past the west bluff, through the Annex and Harrisonville, past the Governor's summer residence and Fort Mackinac, past the east bluff, down Mission Hill, and past Mission Point Resort.

Group Carriage Tour

Group carriage tours are available from Carriage Tours, Inc. (847-3307), on Main Street right across from the Arnold Line Dock. Tickets are $9 for adults and $6 for children, and the tour lasts just under two hours. You'll be transferred from the two-horse, 16-passenger carriage you join in town to a three-horse, 35-passenger carriage for most of the tour.

Your guide will give you a good overview of the island's history and you'll see many of the sights, including Market Street, the Grand Hotel, Arch Rock, Sugar Loaf, and Fort Mackinac. You'll also have a chance to visit Surrey Hill, a shopping area and carriage museum. You can leave the carriage tour at Fort Mackinac, the Grand Hotel, or downtown.

Drive-Yourself Carriage

Jack's Riding Stable (847-3391) on the corner of Market and Cadotte rents carriages that you can drive yourself. Prices range from $24 (for two people) to $36 (for six people).

A drive-yourself carriage is a relaxing way to explore the island's interior.

Take a sense of adventure, this book, some snacks, and your best "giddyup" voice. Drive-yourself carriages are not allowed on Main Street or Market Street. Plan your route from the top of the Grand Hill. The summer homes at the Annex and Fort Holmes are good destinations. There are some hills you should avoid, and they'll tell you about them at Jack's.

TAXI

If "taxi" evokes an image of hailing down a beat-up
Plymouth on a busy street, and speeding from point A to
point B, forget it. Taxis on Mackinac Island are as much
entertainment as they are transportation.

A taxi is a radio-dispatched carriage that seats 12. It is
drawn by two horses and will take you wherever you want
to go... eventually. The route often resembles a milk run,
so plan in advance if you really need to be somewhere at a
specified time (other than "island time").

Taxis operate 24 hours a day, seven days a week. You can
hail one if you're in a busy area, call 847-3323 and request
one, or stop at the dispatch station on Main Street at the
foot of Astor Street. Rates are per person, and vary with
distance. As an example, the charge from downtown to any
hotel except Stonecliffe is $2.50, downtown to Stonecliffe or
the airport is $5.00, and Grand Hotel to Mission Point Resort
is $3.00. (Stated rates are per person, with a minimum of
two people.)

A Horse of Course!

Horses make Mackinac Island work: they taxi visitors from
ferries to hotels, move freight from docks to businesses,
deliver the mail from the plane and boat to the post office,
and even take garbage to the landfill. Horse people who
visit the island are amazed by the skill and diversity of the
550 horses it takes to keep the island working in the
summer.

More than half of the horses are owned by Carriage Tours,
which puts them to work in two- or three-horse team
carriage tours, drays, or taxis. The carriage tour and dray
horses are heavy draft horses, capable of pulling the
weight of a loaded carriage or dray. They are Percheron,
Belgian, and Clydesdale mixes, from the Amish areas of
northern Indiana.

For taxi horses, Carriage Tours looks for lighter, quicker driving horses, usually Standardbreds or Standardbred crosses that aren't quite fast enough to make it on the racing track. The riding stables look for sensible riding horses of mixed breeding.

Horses bound for Mackinac Island make their first stop in Pickford, Michigan, the winter home of the island horses. There they are trained for island duty. The intricate process of carriage horse training begins with breaking one horse to drive, then matching it with an experienced horse. The trainers match the horses' gaits, colors, sizes, and temperaments. Then the team is matched with a driver. (Drivers are selected on the basis of their strength and ability to communicate with horses and people and undergo a minimum of two weeks of training.) The team is ready after the horses are brought to the island and exposed to all sorts of situations that can arise when there are so many horses, bicycles, and people in one location.

Horse lovers sometimes worry that horses on the island are overworked. That is very uncommon. Taxi horses have a four hours on, 12 hours off schedule, while carriage tour horses typically do not work more than five hours a day. The riding stable horses have the longest days, but they are pretty good at making sure their riders don't push them too hard!

Keeping all these horses in footwear is a real challenge. Saddle and taxi horses are shod with steel shoes that have borium tips. Steel shoes alone act like ice skates on pavement, so the borium (an alloy) is added, giving the shoes a cleat effect. The heavier horses are shod with a shoe specially designed for use on the island. It is steel, covered with polyurethane. It is extremely durable, and does not cause as much wear and tear on the roads as the borium shoe does. There are four working blacksmiths on the island in the summer, and one veterinarian.

The best spot for "horse watching" is at the top of the Grand Hotel hill. Grab a seat by the side of the road, and watch all types of horses go by. Then stop at the Grand

Hotel stables (across from the Grand Stand) and check out the draft horses and old carriages. Wander the rest of the way up the hill, past the Carriage Tour barns, to Surrey Hill. It has excellent displays of old carriages and harnesses and photographs of carriages in use. They often have a blacksmith shoeing a horse, and a draft horse out for display.

There are two other unusual horse events to watch for. Look for a dray driver backing a team and a load of freight into a tight loading area. Ask yourself if you could do that in a car! Also look for horses coming over on the ferry. All of the horses arrive on the Arnold Line freight boats. Most of them arrive in May and June, and depart after Labor Day. The day after Labor Day is the busiest, with up to 25 horses on one boat.

Mackinac Island is one of the few places in the country where three-horse hitches are used.

6
BEYOND FUDGE

Mackinac Island's most famous food product is its fudge, but since one cannot live by fudge alone, numerous restaurants serve the tourist and island population. Most are concentrated downtown, and each of the larger hotels has at least one. Most cater to the drop-in visitor, so reservations are rarely required, except where indicated below.

Listings are organized into two sections: downtown restaurants and other locations. Price ranges are based on 1989 lunch and dinner menu pricing and do not include appetizers or beverages. Liquor, children's menus, and air conditioning are noted only where they are available. At the end of the chapter, I've included a list of establishments to check out for nightlife.

If you are hungry and are walking down the street reading this, refer to the map on the next page.

Downtown Restaurants
(shown in **bold** type)

the harbor

Main Street

Carriage House
Iroquois Hotel
Lakeshore Gallery Gifts
Dockside Restaurant
Schwinn Shop
Highstone's Topsider
Dockside T-shirt Shop
Star Line dock
Michelle's Gifts *(upstairs in mall)*
Professor Harry's Photos *(in mall)*
Game Room (in mall)
Ryba's Fudge
Wharf Patio Restaurant
Shepler dock
Orr Kids' Snack Shop
3 Shirts to the Wind
Picture Shop
Village Blacksmith Shop
Bag It *(in mall)*
Forget Me Not Shoppe *(in mall)*
Nyna's Brass *(in mall)*
Harrington's *(in mall)*
Grand Hotel in the Village
Decked Out
Sleeping Turtle
Frank Shama Gifts
Mr. B's
Murdick's Fudge
Baxter's Junk Shop
May's Fudge
Trading Post
Maeve's Art & Antiques
Martha's Sweet Shop
Hardware Store *(coal dock)*
Taxi office
Mighty Mac Hamburgers
Jo Ann's Fudge
Benjamin's
Surrey Sandwich Shop
Carriage Lantern Gifts
Island Shop
Thunderbird Gifts
Arnold dock
Shirts Ahoy *(Arnold dock)*
Waterfront Patio Cafe *(Arnold dock)*
Herbon Pottery *(Arnold dock)*
Indian Drum *(Arnold dock)*
Kilwin's Fudge
Pancake House
Ryba's Fudge
Angel's Sportswear
Pink Pony
Harbor View Dining Room
Chippewa Hotel

French Lane

Hoban Street Cafe

James Cable Dining Room
Lake View Hotel
Pilot House

Hoban Street

Village Inn

Straits Area Wood Products
Balsam Shop
Loon Feather
McNally Cottage
Jo Ann's Fudge
Nephew's
Jesse's Chuck Wagon
Haunted Theatre
Just Seasonal
Kilwin's Fudge
Leather Corral
The Birches
Everybody's Little Mexico
Betty's Gifts
The Big Store
Main St. Old Time Photos
Landing Gull *(in mall)*
Island Scrimshander
Ryba's Fudge
Edward's Gifts

Astor Street Cafe
Mustang Lounge
Little Bob's

Market Street

Astor Street

May's Fudge
Little Great China Restaurant
Ty's Restaurant
Horn's Gaslight Bar
Cookies and Company
Carriage Tours
Chamber of Commerce
Murray Deli and Cocktail Lounge
Murray Hotel Dining Room
Murray Hotel
Murdick's Fudge
3 Brothers Sarducci
Shirt Tales
Mackinac Trader
Alford's Drug Store
Island Bookstore *(upstairs)*
Marilyn's Hair Studio *(upstairs)*
Doud's Mercantile

Silver Mine

Fort Street

DOWNTOWN RESTAURANTS

(Listed in order as you stroll on Main Street beginning at the corner of Main and Fort, on the north side, with the south side (lake side) of Main next. Restaurants on streets adjoining Main and Market follow. See map.)

Restaurants on the north side of Main Street
---

3 BROTHERS SARDUCCI
Lunch and dinner. $3 - $8. No credit cards.

Mackinac's answer to Tom Monaghan, the 3 Brothers even deliver (sometimes, depending on how much help they have!). In addition to pizza, 3 Brothers Sarducci sells calzones and Italian submarine sandwiches, and they'd be glad to package them for a picnic in the park.

MURRAY HOTEL DINING ROOM
847-3361
Dinner. $6 - $11. Visa and Master Card accepted. Liquor available. Children's menu.

When the season gets into full swing, the Murray Hotel opens its dining room and serves American food, family-style. The favorites are fried chicken and prime rib.

MURRAY DELI AND COCKTAIL LOUNGE
847-3354
Breakfast, lunch and dinner. $3 - $8. No credit cards. Liquor available. Children's menu.

A cross between a genuine New York-style deli, a hotel restaurant, and a downtown lounge, featuring a long picture window looking over Main Street, the Murray Deli is a unique experience. At breakfast, select your food from the buffet or from a small menu. For lunch or dinner, order one of their 50 named sandwiches on homemade bread ("Bo Schembeefler," "Chick Mate," "Cheese Be Seated"), a pizza, a chicken dinner, or your basic BLT, to eat in or to go. Go right up to the counter when you walk in;

this is a self-service deli.   Afterwards, enjoy the frozen yogurt bar.

COOKIES AND COMPANY
847-3811
Lunch, dinner, and late-night snacks. $2 - $3.   No credit cards.

Cookies and Company is a good place when you have a case of the munchies.   Its self-service menu includes pizza by the slice, hot dogs, homemade cookies and breads, and ice cream.

HORN'S GASLIGHT BAR
847-6154
Lunch, dinner, and late-night snacks. $2 - $8. Visa   and Master Card accepted. Liquor available.   Air conditioned.

Better known as one of the island night spots, Horn's Gaslight Bar and Grill is also a good spot to get a quick sandwich, burrito, or hamburger.   During the day, you can sing along with Tom and Jerry.   At night, it's a great spot to watch or participate in the eclectic dancing scene with islanders, summer workers, tourists, and conventioneers. You enter Horn's onto the dance floor, so be prepared to dance your way to a table.   If you are fortunate, the world famous Shawn Reilly Band will be playing a gig at Horn's when you're on the island.   Before you know it, you might be on stage!

TY'S RESTAURANT
847-3426
Breakfast, lunch, dinner, and late-night snacks. $1 - $4. No credit cards.   Liquor available.

If you're looking for an inexpensive meal on the run, Ty's is a good bet.   The menu is primarily sandwiches, burgers, hotdogs, and chicken, served in baskets with french fries.

LITTLE GREAT CHINA RESTAURANT
Lunch and dinner. $1 - $5.   No credit cards.   Air conditioned.

Little Great China is the island's only Chinese restaurant. It has a small menu of Chinese and American fare to eat in or carry out. It's a good option for a quick and inexpensive meal.

Over 40 restaurants serve a wide range of meals during the summer season.

EVERYBODY'S LITTLE MEXICO
847-3274
Lunch and dinner. Entrees $6 - $9. No credit cards. Liquor available. Air conditioned. Children's menu.

Only on Mackinac Island would the Mexican restaurant feature a blend of Victorian and southwestern decor! Everybody's serves up huge portions of Americanized Mexican food in a pleasant environment. Its "Macho Nachos" may be one of the best buys on the island; the $7 appetizer was enough for two of us for dinner.

JESSE'S CHUCK WAGON
847-3775
Breakfast, lunch, early dinner (closes at 6 p.m.). $4 - $8. No credit cards. Air conditioned.

Mackinac's answer to the 1950's diner, Jesse's is the place to go to get some local color and inexpensive eggs and coffee or BLT and lemonade. Most of the seating is along a counter, where you can watch Jesse cook your meal.

PILOT HOUSE - LAKE VIEW HOTEL
847-3384
Lunch and dinner. $4 - $16. Visa and Master Card accepted. Liquor available. Air conditioned.

The Pilot House is a large, family-style restaurant serving sandwiches and more substantial American fare. It also has a soup and salad bar. Its window seats are a great place for people watching.

JAMES CABLE DINING ROOM - LAKE VIEW HOTEL
847-3384
Breakfast, lunch, and dinner. Dinner $12 - $25. American Express, Visa, and Master Card accepted. Liquor available. Air conditioned. Reservations required. Children's menu.

The Lake View Hotel's James Cable Dining Room serves regional cuisine in a formal (for Mackinac) setting. Try the veal picatta or the seafood in a pastry. Window seats overlooking Main Street are great fun, particularly as the night goes on!

Restaurants on the south side (lake side) of Main Street, beginning at Marquette Park

---

HARBOR VIEW DINING ROOM - CHIPPEWA HOTEL
847-3341
Breakfast, lunch, and dinner. Lunch $4 - $6, dinner $10 - $16. American Express, Visa, and Master Card accepted. Liquor available. Air conditioned. Reservations suggested for dinner. Children's menu.

With its beautiful view of the Straits and the harbor's activity, this restaurant earns its name. It is one of the most popular places on the island for breakfast. The Harbor View is a bargain, and the Eggs Benedict are great. For an outdoor lunch, try the pool side patio. (Lunch service also available inside.) At dinner enjoy the whitefish (you specify the preparation) or the chicken and shrimp Dijon.

PINK PONY - CHIPPEWA HOTEL
847-3341
Lunch. $4 - $6. American Express, Visa and Master Card accepted. Liquor available. Air conditioned.

Adjacent to the Chippewa Hotel lobby, the Pink Pony is a charming oak-panelled lounge. It has limited booth and table seating and a long bar with a television. There is entertainment on summer weekends (pop/easy listening). It has a limited appetizer menu and serves the same luncheon menu as the Harbor View Dining Room. During the yacht races, sailors who have completed the race pack the place so you'll need to take a number to get in!

Some visitors still prefer fudge.

PANCAKE HOUSE AND SANDWICH SHOP
847-3829
*Breakfast, lunch, and early dinner. $3 - $6 No credit cards.
Air conditioned.*

For an inexpensive breakfast in a plain wrapper, the Pancake House is a good choice. It offers breakfast fare all day, and adds a sandwich menu at lunch and dinner.

WATERFRONT PATIO CAFE
Lunch. $2 - $4. No credit cards.

On the Arnold Line Dock, the Waterfront Patio Cafe has sandwiches, hot dogs, and burgers, served at tables outside.

SURREY SANDWICH SHOP
847-3743
Lunch, dinner, and late-night snacks. $3 - $8. American Express, Master Card, Visa, and Discover accepted.

For a quick submarine sandwich, it's hard to beat the Surrey Sandwich Shop. It also offers other sandwiches, salads, and homemade chili. Call and they'll prepare a huge picnic for your group.

MIGHTY MAC HAMBURGERS
847-3813
Lunch, dinner, and late-night snacks. $2 - $3. No credit cards.

Mackinac Island is one place that Ronald McDonald hasn't discovered, so your kids will learn to like Mighty Mac's charbroiled hamburgers. They also serve hot dogs and salads. Limited seating.

MARTHA'S SWEET SHOP
847-3790
Breakfast, sweets. $1 - $2. No credit cards. Carry-out only.

If you follow the early morning traffic, you're likely to end up at Martha's for one of her famous melt-in-your-mouth cinnamon rolls and large cups of coffee. Martha also makes muffins, brownies and cookies, and sells ice cream. With advance notice, she will bake a cake for a special occasion.

MR B'S
Lunch and dinner. $1 - $3. No credit cards.

Mackinac's version of the Dairy Queen, Mr. B's serves ice cream treats, hot dogs, nachos and other items from its window on Main Street. Picnic tables are available outside in back.

ORR KIDS' SNACK SHOP
Snacks and lunch. $1 - $2. No credit cards. Carry-out only.

Orr Kids' has hot dogs, nachos, bratwurst, ice cream, popcorn, and cotton candy conveniently located next to its bicycle rental shop.

THE WHARF PATIO RESTAURANT
Snacks and lunch. $2 - $4. No credit cards.

Right next to the Shepler Dock, the Wharf has picnic tables and walk-up service for hamburgers, nachos, polish sausage, and such. If you want ice cream, go next door, to Wharf Waffles and Cones.

DOCKSIDE RESTAURANT
Breakfast, lunch, and dinner. $3 - $6. No credit cards.

At the far western end of town, Dockside serves up pancakes and eggs in the morning, and sandwiches, subs, burgers, and soup until 6:00 p.m.

CARRIAGE HOUSE - IROQUOIS HOTEL
847-3321
Lunch and dinner. Lunch $6 - $12; dinner $15 - $20. Visa and Master Card accepted. Liquor available. Reservations recommended for dinner. Children's menu.

The Carriage House is on most residents' list of "must dos." The view of the Straits is remarkable and the food and service are impressive. It has two rooms, one more traditional and the other with a garden feel. I particularly enjoy sitting on the terrace, if the weather permits, and watching the boats go by as I eat.

Favorites are the grilled seafood salad sandwich for lunch, and whitefish, filet mignon or prime rib for dinner.

Desserts are made fresh daily; the Mackinac Island Fudge
Ice Cream Puff is a personal favorite.

| Restaurants on streets adjoining Main and Market Street |

ASTOR STREET CAFE
847-3252
*On Astor Street. Lunch. $4 - $6. Visa and Master Card
accepted. Air conditioned. Children's menu.*

An old-fashioned ice cream parlor turned restaurant, Astor
Street Cafe has managed the transition well. My favorites
are still the ice cream specialities, but burgers and
sandwiches are good too. If you call in advance, they'll
handle a large group lunch to go. If you want an ice
cream cone to go, stop at their window to the left of the
Cafe entrance.

MUSTANG LOUNGE
847-9916
*On Astor Street. Lunch and dinner. $3 - $8. No credit
cards. Liquor available.*

The Mustang is the only restaurant that is open year-
round. It's a great spot for a cheap hamburger and a
Stroh's, and a sense of what winter on Mackinac Island
might be like. There's a television and an old jukebox in
the corner. After the crush of the tourist season passes,
they move the pool table back in.

LITTLE BOB'S RESTAURANT
847-3512
*On Astor Street at the corner of Market. Breakfast, lunch
and dinner. Lunch $5 - $8; dinner $8 - $16. American
Express, Visa, and Master Card accepted. Liquor available.
Air conditioned. Children's menu.*

Go to Little Bob's with a hearty appetite. It's a traditional
family-style restaurant with large portions and an
optional all-you-can-eat buffet on Sunday mornings and

most evenings. At breakfast have a giant cinnamon roll or the newly introduced oat bran muffins. Dinner entrees include whitefish, barbecue ribs, stir-fry and the like.

VILLAGE INN
847-3542
On Hoban Street. Lunch, dinner, and late-night snacks. Dinner entrees $9 - $16. Visa and Master Card accepted. Liquor available. Air conditioned.

The "VI," as insiders call it, is a favorite watering hole for island business people, and is also an excellent spot for moderately priced, cozy family dining. Whitefish every way is the speciality (smoked whitefish appetizer, whitefish chowder and three types of whitefish are on the menu). The planked whitefish, which is baked on an oak plank and surrounded by mashed potatoes, is outstanding. The chicken and shrimp Dijon is also a favorite. Burgers, nachos and the like are also available. Expect a wait on big sports days because the big screen TV is popular.

Kid's Corner

Mackinac Island is an ideal family vacation destination. All the hotels, restaurants, and shops welcome children. You won't have any trouble finding high chairs or hot dogs, cribs or cots. And older children love the freedom that comes with not needing to wait for mom or dad to drive them anywhere! There's plenty to keep kids of all ages busy. Some favorites:

Picnics -- Load your bicycle basket with sandwiches and soda and pedal to a special picnic area.

Fort Mackinac -- Kids can play soldier on a grand scale. The musket and cannon firings are great crowd pleasers. And check out the children's discovery room, where children explore the sounds, sights, and feel of history.

Swimming -- From swimming holes to swimming pools, it's all explained in Chapter Ten.

Playgrounds -- There are playgrounds at the school, behind the Indian Dormitory, and at Great Turtle Park. Marquette Park, Windermere Point, Mission Point, and the grounds behind Fort Mackinac are good for running, jumping, and playing outdoor games.

Horses -- Most kids love horses. Carriage tours, taxi rides, drive-yourself carriages, and saddle horses are all popular with the younger set. Most carriage drivers will let you pet the horses or pose for a picture, but ask them first.

Biking -- Family bicycle outings are easy and safe. There are lots of bikes for rent that are geared to children. See Chapter Five.

Competition -- During the Lilac Festival and Independence Day celebrations (see page 5), there are competitive games for children, including foot races, sack races, and greased pole competitions.

Haunted Theater -- A favorite with the teenagers, the Haunted Theater is on the west end of town, the north side. Even if you wait outside, you'll be able to hear the screams.

Arcade Games -- If pinball or Pac-Man fever strikes, check the list on page 146.

Movies -- Monday night is movie night on the island. Family movies are shown at Mission Point Resort. Check the *Town Crier* or the Chamber of Commerce for information.

Babysitting -- Locating a baby-sitter can sometimes be a challenge. Check with your hotel or the Chamber of Commerce for referrals.

Strollers -- Strollers can be rented from Orr Kids' Bicycle Rental on the west end of town, south side.

HOBAN STREET CAFE -LAKE VIEW HOTEL
847-3384
On Hoban Street. Lunch. $5 - $7. American Express, Visa, and Master Card accepted. Liquor available.

Mackinac's street side outdoor cafe, the Hoban Street Cafe is around the corner from the Lake View Hotel on the west end of town. The fare is sandwiches, soups, and salads.

OTHER LOCATIONS

TEA ROOM - FORT MACKINAC
Lunch. $5 - $9. Visa and Master Card accepted.

For a bird's eye view of the harbor, enjoy lunch or dessert at the Tea Room at Fort Mackinac. Run by the Grand Hotel, the Tea Room serves soups, salads, and sandwiches outside under umbrellas, or inside. You must pay admission to Fort Mackinac to eat at the Tea Room (see page 110).

GUVNER'S TABLE - ISLAND HOUSE HOTEL
847-3347
Breakfast and dinner. $15 - $21. Visa and Master Card accepted. Liquor available. Air Conditioned. Children's menu.

In the oldest hotel on the island, the Guvner's Table blends a traditional black and red decor with a harbor view and pleasant entertainment. Specialities include roast duckling, whitefish, and surf and turf.

THE PUB AT HARBOR PARK
847-3454
Lunch and dinner. Lunch $5 - $7; dinner $11 - $16. Visa and Master Card accepted. Liquor available. Children's menu.

The Pub at Harbor Park is a favorite among locals and boaters because of its location away from downtown, just east of the marina. Windows along two sides afford excellent harbor views. The food is good, and the atmosphere is warm.

OYSTER BAR AT HARBOR PARK
847-3501
Lunch, dinner, and late-night snacks. $3 - $13. Visa and Master Card accepted. Liquor available.

The Oyster Bar is the place to go if you like steamers with your Stroh's. In this tiny bar at the east end of the marina, oysters, clams, shrimp, and sandwiches are the fare. Some days, they add an outdoor barbecue with chicken, seafood and steak kebobs. At night, it's a hangout for the college-age crowd, but don't let that scare you away. The Oyster Bar is a pearl in the rough.

ROUND ISLAND BAR AND GRILL - MISSION POINT RESORT
847-3312
Lunch and dinner. $4 - $8. Visa and Master Card accepted. Liquor available. Air conditioned.

For a casual lunch and some freighter watching, the Round Island Bar and Grill at Mission Point Resort is a great bet. Sit around the circular bar, at one of the tables around the hotel lounge, or on the terrace when weather permits. Service is also available near the pool when the weather is nice. Easy listening entertainment most nights.

POINT DINING ROOM - MISSION POINT RESORT
847-3312
Breakfast and dinner. $16 - $25. Visa and Master Card accepted. Liquor available. Reservations suggested for dinner. Air conditioned.

The Point Dining Room at Mission Point Resort has a vaulted pine ceiling, pink and green decor, and a beautiful view of the Straits. A piano player performs most evenings. Dinner favorites include Veal Victorian or whitefish, followed by the Swan Lake Mousse. Breakfast is either a buffet or from the menu; call ahead to find out.

FRENCH OUTPOST
847-3772
On Cadotte Avenue, across from the Little Stone Church. Lunch, dinner, and late-night snacks. $3 - $9 Visa and Master Card accepted. Liquor available.

The "OP" is a rustic restaurant during the day and a hopping rock-n-roll spot at night.   Its menu is primarily soups, salad, pizza, and sandwiches; or you can enjoy oysters or clams from the raw bar.   It serves in three areas: the main restaurant, the screened-in porch, or the deck overlooking the Straits and the Grand Hotel golf course. For a very special occasion, order the "Yachty Special": chicken wings and a bottle of Dom Perignon for $100.05.

CANNONBALL
Snacks and lunch. $1 - $4.   No credit cards.   Carry-out only.

The Cannonball is the best place to eat if you get hungry and are halfway around the island.   In fact, it is the only place.   At British Landing, the Cannonball has soda, snacks, sandwiches, and hot dogs for tired bikers.

RON'S MOM'S COOKIES
At Surrey Hills Square, at the top of the Grand Hotel past the Carriage Tour barns. Snacks. $1 - $2.   No credit cards.

Take some cookies with you on your carriage tour, or save them   for   after   dinner!   Ron's   Mom   even   thoughtfully provides milk.

FEEDBAG
847-3593
At Surrey Hills Square, at the top of the Grand Hotel past the Carriage Tour barns. Lunch. $1 - $3.   No credit cards.

Enjoy soup, sandwiches or a burger while you wander through the Surrey Hill carriage displays or sit at picnic tables inside or outside.

Grand Hotel Restaurants

In order to eat breakfast or lunch at any of the Grand Hotel restaurants, except the Grand Stand and the Pool Grill, you'll need to pay the $5/person hotel admission charge. The charge is credited to your bill if you eat lunch in the Main Dining Room. At night, the hotel does not charge an admission fee, but all guests must meet the hotel dress code (men - coat and tie, women - dress or dressy pant suit). The dress code at the Grand Stand is slightly more relaxed, but jeans are not allowed. Tipping is not allowed at the Grand Hotel.

MAIN DINING ROOM - GRAND HOTEL
847-3331
Breakfast, lunch, and dinner. Buffet lunch $19.50, dinner $40. Visa and Master Card accepted. Liquor available. Air conditioned. Children's menu.

For a step into the Victorian days of extravagant dressing and multi-course meals, the Grand's Main Dining Room at dinner cannot be beaten. Guests are ushered in down a runway surrounded by pillars and mirrors that was designed as a fashion parade. The orchestra plays, and you'll order from a rotating menu of five-course dinners. Lunch is also unique, with ten banquet tables filled with hot and cold entrees, salads, and breads. I spend most of my time at the dessert tables, where 30 different creations are available daily.

TERRACE ROOM - GRAND HOTEL
847-3331
Entertainment, dancing, and drinks. Visa and Master Card accepted. Air conditioned.

The Grand's Terrace Room has the best dance floor on Mackinac Island. It is roomy, and with entertainers playing big band style and rotating on the band stand, it is usually active.

AUDUBON BAR - GRAND HOTEL
847-3331

Hors d'oeuvres and drinks. Visa and Master Card accepted. Air conditioned.

With its dark green and maroon decor and nature theme, the Audubon Bar has an exclusive hunt club feel. Its quiet, comfortable atmosphere is a welcome retreat from the afternoon and evening activity of the rest of the hotel.

POOL GRILL - GRAND HOTEL
847-3331
Lunch. $4 - $7. Visa and Master Card accepted.

If you are headed for the Grand Hotel pool, plan to stay for lunch. The grill is fired up, and you can have a hotdog, hamburger, or a grilled chicken sandwich. If you are not a guest of the hotel, you must pay the $6/person pool fee.

CARLETON'S TEA STORE - GRAND HOTEL
Lunch. $4 - $8. Visa and Master Card are accepted. Air conditioned.

Tucked into a hallway at the Grand Hotel, Carleton's offers a limited menu of soups, sandwiches, and fruit and cheese trays, and an outstanding array of desserts. Lunch or dessert at Carleton's is a wonderful, affordable way to experience the Grand.

"While on the island seek out the Grand Hotel museum rooms which display photographs, documents, maps, magazine and newspaper articles and small artifacts concerning Grand Hotel and island...

My favorite spot for dinner is the east-most table on the terrace of The Grand Stand at Grand golf course. The sirloin steak is great, and if I've skipped lunch that day I add the thick onion soup in a crock. For dessert, the Grand Hotel pecan ball, of course..."

W. T. Rabe
Photojournalist and public relations consultant
Organizer of Mackinac Island Stone Skipping Tournament

GRAND STAND - GRAND HOTEL GROUNDS
847-3331
Lunch and dinner. Lunch $5 - $7; dinner $6 - $16. Visa and Master Card accepted. Liquor available. Children's menu.

The Grand Stand is located on the Grand Hotel golf course and serves soup, salad, and sandwiches at lunch inside and outside under umbrella tables. It's a great spot to watch the carriage tours and golfers go by. In the evening, the Grand Stand adds more substantial fare and often has entertainment. On some nights, you can enjoy jazz under the stars. The folks at the Grand Stand will also prepare a picnic box lunch to go for you if you call in advance.

GERANIUM BAR - GRAND HOTEL
847-3331
Continental breakfast and lunch. Lunch $6 - $14. Visa and Master Card accepted. Liquor available. Air conditioned. Children's menu.

If you don't want to eat in the Grand's Main Dining Room, the Geranium Bar serves elegant meals ala carte. Add an excellent view of the Straits and you are on your way to a good day.

CUPOLA BAR - GRAND HOTEL
847-3331
Entertainment, dancing, and drinks. Visa and Master Card accepted. Not air conditioned.

The Grand recently turned the cupola on the top of the hotel into a bar, and it is a great addition to the island's nightlife. It's a two-story bar, with a dance floor on one level and the band playing jazz, pop, or easy listening on the other. With its commanding view of the Straits and a carnival feeling, the Cupola Bar is a fun place to spend an evening.

NIGHTLIFE

The nightlife on Mackinac Island is certainly more limited than that of a large city, but for its size, the island has a lot of action after the sun goes down. Following is a list of establishments that are usually open late during the high season, along with notes about whether they have entertainment or food. Those that have a * also serve alcoholic beverages. All of them are more completely described above. The list below follows the order of the descriptions above.

Cookies and Company - late-night snacks.
*Horn's Gaslight Bar - entertainment, dancing, and late-night snacks.
*Ty's Restaurant - late-night snacks.
*Pink Pony - entertainment.
  Surrey Sandwich Shop - late-night snacks.
  Mighty Mac Hamburgers - late-night snacks.
*Mustang Lounge - late-night snacks.
*Village Inn - late-night snacks.
*Round Island Bar and Grill - entertainment and late-night snacks.
*Guvner's Lounge - entertainment.
*Oyster Bar - late-night snacks.
*French Outpost - entertainment, dancing, and late-night snacks.
*Terrace Room - Grand Hotel - entertainment and dancing.
*Audubon Bar - Grand Hotel
*Grand Stand - Grand Hotel - entertainment, dancing (some nights), and late-night snacks.
*Geranium Bar - Grand Hotel
*Cupola Bar - Grand Hotel - entertainment, dancing, and late-night snacks.
*Stonecliffe -- entertainment some nights.

7
T-SHIRTS, TOMAHAWKS, AND TREASURES

Time was on Mackinac Island when about all you could purchase was a pound of fudge and a rubber-tipped tomahawk. Those time-honored traditions still exist, but the shopping scene has expanded greatly in the last two decades. Now the diligent shopper can find all sorts of ways to spend money -- fudge, T-shirts, fine clothing, handmade baskets, watercolors, jewelry, etc. But you'll find no franchised stores, because local ordinance prohibits them.

There are three primary shopping districts: 1) Main Street between Fort Street and French Lane; 2) Market Street between Fort Street and French Lane and the side streets connecting Main and Market Street; and 3) the Grand Hotel shops. There are also a few shops in other island locations, as described at the end of this chapter.

Because there is so much to see on the island, and you won't want to spend all day shopping, I've included short descriptions of each shop to help you plan your time.

Main Street Shops
(shown in **bold** type)

Carriage House
Iroquois Hotel
Lakeshore Gallery Gifts
Dockside Restaurant
Schwinn Shop
Highstone's Topsider
Dockside T-shirt Shop
Star Line dock
Michelle's Gifts (upstairs in mall)
Professor Harry's Photos (in mall)
Game Room (in mall)
Ryba's Fudge
Wharf Patio Restaurant
Shepler dock
Orr Kids' Snack Shop
3 Shirts to the Wind
Picture Shop
Village Blacksmith Shop
Bag It (in mall)
Forget Me Not Shoppe (in mall)
Nyna's Brass (in mall)
Harrington's (in mall)
Grand Hotel in the Village
Decked Out
Sleeping Turtle
Frank Shama Gifts
Mr. B's
Murdick's Fudge
Baxter's Junk Shop
May's Fudge
Trading Post
Maeve's Art & Antiques
Martha's Sweet Shop
Hardware Store (coal dock)
Taxi office
Mighty Mac Hamburgers
Jo Ann's Fudge
Benjamin's
Surrey Sandwich Shop
Carriage Lantern Gifts
Island Shop
Thunderbird Gifts
Arnold dock
Shirts Ahoy (Arnold dock)
Waterfront Patio Cafe (Arnold dock)
Herbon Pottery (Arnold dock)
Indian Drum (Arnold dock)
Kilwin's Fudge
Pancake House
Ryba's Fudge
Angel's Sportswear
Pink Pony
Harbor View Dining Room
Chippewa Hotel

the harbor

Main Street

Market Street

French Lane

James Cable Dining Room
Lake View Hotel
Pilot House

Hoban Street

Straits Area Wood Products
Balsam Shop
Loon Feather
McNally Cottage
Jo Ann's Fudge
Nephew's
Jesse's Chuck Wagon
Haunted Theatre
Just Seasonal
Kilwin's Fudge
Leather Corral
The Birches
Everybody's Little Mexico
Betty's Gifts
The Big Store
Main Street Old Time Photos (in mall)
Landing Gull (in mall)
Island Scrimshander
Ryba's Fudge
Edward's Gifts

Astor Street

May's Fudge
Little Great China Restaurant
Ty's Restaurant
Horn's Gaslight Bar
Cookies and Company
Carriage Tours
Chamber of Commerce
Murray Deli and Cocktail Lounge
Murray Hotel Dining Room
Murray Hotel
Murdick's Fudge
3 Brothers Sarducci
Shirt Tales
Mackinac Trader
Alford's Drug Store
Island Bookstore (upstairs)
Marilyn's Hair Studio (upstairs)
Doud's Mercantile

Fort Street

MAIN STREET SHOPPING

Listed in order as you stroll down Main Street beginning at the corner of Main and Fort Street. The north side is listed first, followed by the south side (lake side) of Main Street. (See the map.)

Shops on the north side of Main Street

DOUD'S MERCANTILE

Doud's is the island's only grocery store and has been serving island residents and tourists since the 1840's. Steven Doud's grandfather came to the island during that period, escaping the potato famine in Ireland. For a small town grocery, it has a wide selection. Open all year.

MARILYN'S HAIR STUDIO

Marilyn is located above Doud's, and she is one of two hair stylists on the island (the other is at the Grand Hotel). She'll do all the basics for both men and women and is a favorite with the local folk.

ISLAND BOOKSTORE

A wonderful spot for a rainy day, the Island Bookstore carries new and used books in paperback and hardcover. It has a fine selection of regional books, as well as the usual best-sellers, children's books, mysteries and romance novels.

ALFORD'S DRUG STORE

Another island institution, Alford's has been dispensing prescriptions and other necessary items to island residents and visitors for years. They are accustomed to travelers who forget their medications, and they also have a wide variety of souvenirs and gift items. Open all year.

MACKINAC TRADER

The Mackinac Trader is a peddler's combination of clothing, jewelry, and home accessories. They carry a wide variety of cotton and wool sweaters and some unusual clothing. Excellent prices on fine silver jewelry. Exotic women's belts. Beautiful dhurrie rugs and wall hangings.

SHIRT TALES

In addition to the island's most extensive selection of quality T-shirts, Shirt Tales carries contemporary casual clothes for men and women. You'll also find jackets, sweatshirts, and rain gear here.

MURDICK'S FUDGE -- See page 89.

MAY'S FUDGE -- See page 89.

EDWARD'S GIFTS AND SOUVENIRS

Primarily a souvenir shop, Edward's can surprise the diligent shopper with its collection of bone china and Hummel figurines. It also carries shoes, raincoats, and hats for those caught on the island without the essentials.

RYBA'S FUDGE -- See page 90.

ISLAND SCRIMSHANDER

A resident artist meticulously creates island and nautical scenes on ivory and fashions them into necklaces, earrings, rings, knives, pen sets, belt buckles, and more. The artist, Gary Kiracofe, is a year-round resident. His brothers have scrimshaw shops in the east.

LANDING GULL (in the mall behind the Scrimshander)

The Landing Gull offers an eclectic mixture of nautical gifts, Michigan artwork, and basic souvenirs. Its Michigan works include Great Lakes sand castles and ceramic sea gulls and cookbooks. It also has some attractive Mackinac Island photo note cards, prints, posters, and watercolors.

MAIN STREET OLD TIME PHOTOS (in the mall behind the Scrimshander)

Slip on a costume from the collection and find yourself in the 19th century as a military man, a huckster, a Victorian lady, or a hussy! Photos are developed in authentic looking brown tones while you wait. Remember, don't smile!

THE BIG STORE

A souvenir lover's delight, the Big Store is the biggest of the traditional island shops. It carries all the favorites: T-shirts, sweatshirts, tomahawks, hats, wind-up toy, and other trinkets.

BETTY'S GIFTS

Walk right in off the street; Betty's hospitable shop has no doors to block the activity. Look for the cutlery case that contains fine quality knives for fishing, hunting, and hiking use. Glittering along the back wall are cut glass stemmed tumblers. There are also souvenirs of every description.

THE BIRCHES

The Birches carries a large selection of Indian toys, as well as knives, jewelry, hats, and other souvenir items.

LEATHER CORRAL

As the name implies, the Leather Corral specializes in leather goods, including wallets and purses, moccasins, belts, and duffel bags. It also has numerous horse figurines, Indian toys, and Indian bead necklaces.

KILWIN'S FUDGE AND GIFTS -- See page 89.

JUST SEASONAL

The owners of Just Seasonal have done an excellent job creating a unique store around the seasonal theme. They have a large selection of Christmas items, including decorations displayed on trees, large caroler figurines, and unusual Christmas candles. In the fall they feature Halloween decorations. They also have a varied collection of Island theme watercolors, music boxes and German cuckoo clocks.

NEPHEW'S OF MACKINAC ISLAND

Nephew's is the place to go when you didn't pack quite the right clothes for a special outing. It is a full-line clothing store for men and women featuring Liz Claiborne, Ralph Lauren, Adrienne Vittadini, Sperry Topsider, and others.

JOANN'S FUDGE -- See page 89.

LOON FEATHER

The Loon Feather has an extensive selection of pewter figurine collectibles. In addition to the usual moccasins and sweatshirts, it carries Hudson Bay woolens, stuffed animals, sweaters, and lots of inexpensive jewelry. A new item is the Victorian cowboy hat. Don't scoff, try one on!

BALSAM SHOP

Most of the people in the Balsam Shop seem to be there to buy film or play one of the arcade games in the center of the store. It has the souvenir mainstays -- T-shirts, hats, knives, and Indian trinkets. Its also has a larger-than-most selection of Mackinac Island trays, mugs, trivets and the like.

STRAITS AREA WOOD PRODUCTS

Straits Area Wood Products will create a personalized sign, box, or other wood product for you while you continue your pursuit of the best fudge on the island.

Shops on the south side of Main Street,
beginning at Main and Fort

ANGEL'S SPORTSWEAR

Angel's has found its niche as an importer of unusual handmade sweaters and clothing. Wool sweaters from Iceland and hand knit leather sweaters from Turkey are the show stoppers, but they also carry a variety of sweaters, baskets, and bags from all over. Angel's also carries moderately priced shorts, cotton shirts, sunglasses, and Mackinac Island insignia polo shirts.

Most of the shops are on Main Street.

RYBA'S FUDGE -- See page 90.

KILWIN'S FUDGE -- See page 89.

INDIAN DRUM

The Indian Drum derived its name from its authentic Indian-made replicas of Indian tools and instruments. It also has a large collection of red flannel shirts, nightshirts, and other clothing from the Original Cedar Springs (Michigan) Red Flannel Factory. The other walls are filled with pipes and tobacco, beer steins, brass knickknacks, large baskets, backpacks, and ladies' bags.

HERBON HANDMADE STONEWARE POTTERY

This is a small, charming shop, tucked away on the Arnold Line Dock and filled with lamps, bowls, platters, and other pottery. Most feature floral designs in blues, pinks, and purples. Prices are moderate for handmade stoneware.

SHIRTS AHOY

The name says it all -- a shop on the edge of the water loaded with T-shirts of all kinds.

THUNDERBIRD GIFTS

Owned by the same merchant as the Island Shop next door, this store is mainly T-shirts. Look along the front wall for some jewelry items and a whole case of crushed coral necklaces. Some ivory pieces and scrimshaw can be found here too.

ISLAND SHOP

Barely visible through the window are ceramic cats and bunnies. A vast display of T-shirts and sweatshirts that boast of Mackinac Island makes up the majority of the Island Shop. But tucked in corners are ceramics, miniature animals, and larger figurines.

CARRIAGE LANTERN GIFTS

Carriage Lantern Gifts features a large selection of inexpensive jewelry, including nautical theme pieces and charms. Its Mackinac Island insignia items include ashtrays, hats, mugs, T-shirts, trivets, magnets, and a small selection of Christmas ornaments.

BENJAMIN'S OF MACKINAC ISLAND

Benjamin's biggest sellers are camera-related products -- film, film processing, batteries, cameras, camera cases, and even video film -- but a wander through Benjamin's can uncover many gift and souvenir items. Its Mackinac Island photo album and book collection is unusual, as is its collection of mobiles, wind chimes, and bird feeders. Don't miss the antique island post cards, which are tucked in among the Mackinac Island bridge tallies and carriage motif napkins. You can rent a camera for $5/day if you forgot yours.

JOANN'S FUDGE -- See page 89.

HARDWARE STORE

Operated by the folks at the Arnold Line, this place hums with activity spring, summer, and fall. From massive renovation supplies to the little screw that fell out of the toilet paper holder, Lee carries it in his surprisingly complete hardware store.

MAEVE'S ARTS AND ANTIQUES

After spending many summers on the island as a child, Maeve decided to join the ranks of merchants seeking to upgrade the island shopping experience. She has created a colorful, creative, fun shop. Her contemporary jewelry collection (or is it art? or both?) is unmatched on the island; the rest of the shop is a menagerie of handmade items, including toys, ceramics, baskets, boxes, small watercolors, kaleidoscopes, and other treasures.

TRADING POST

If you let your young children in the Trading Post, you'll probably lose them for hours; it is filled with the trinkets kids love to inspect. Miniature everything, Indian toys, rubber spiders, oversized sunglasses, unusual belt buckles, you name it. It also has the souvenir shop's array of Mackinac Island hats, T-shirts, mugs, beach towels, pot holders and place mats.

MAY'S FUDGE -- See page 89.

BAXTER'S JUNK SHOP

As the name implies, the items offered here will appeal to a child's sense of Mackinac souvenirs. Part of a family-owned triumvirate of similar island stores, Baxter's had a moment of glory in the movie "Somewhere in Time," when it was called Baxter's Coin Shop and was featured in the street scene.

MURDICK'S FUDGE -- See page 89.

FRANK SHAMA GIFTS

Now operated by Frank Shama's daughter and son-in-law, the Frank Shama Shop has been in existence on Mackinac Island over 35 years. A vast selection of Royal Doulton mugs lines the shelves above the souvenirs. While the most popular item is probably the tom-tom, the owners are justifiably proud of their fine china items.

SLEEPING TURTLE

The Sleeping Turtle is a combination stationery and gift shop, with a dash of souvenir thrown in. It has a large selection of cards and stationery, beautiful baskets made by the Winnebago Indian tribe in Wisconsin, candles, windsocks and cotton and wool handwoven throw rugs. For good measure, it also has a small selection of T-shirts and sweatshirts. Look for the island design needlepoint kits.

DECKED OUT

Featuring moderately priced men's and women's casual clothes, Decked Out can be counted on for the latest colors and designs in comfortable wear. They also have rain wear and a selection of Sperry Topsider shoes. If you are looking for a Mackinac memento to wear but don't want a T-shirt, you might enjoy their polo shirts and sweaters.

GRAND HOTEL IN THE VILLAGE

For those day-trippers who do not take the walk up to the Grand, the Grand has provided a little taste downtown. From the dark green and white decor to the scent of fine soaps and potpourri, this store feels grand. It's a collection of Grand Hotel paraphernalia (robes, slippers, sweatshirts, hats, teapots, and glasses), high quality children's toys, Mackinac Island and Grand Hotel books, and other gifts. The merchandise is generally pricey. There is a sister store on Market Street; the Market Street store focuses more on bath products and linens.

HARRINGTON'S (in the mall behind Grand Hotel in the Village)

Harrington's features fine quality leather goods -- purses, gloves, moccasins, and key chains -- and other handmade gifts such as blown glass ornaments and vases, inlaid wooden boxes, and Indian-made pillows and rugs.

NYNA'S BRASS (in the mall)

Wear your sunglasses when you walk into Nyna's or you'll be overcome by all the gleaming brass pieces. Nyna carries a huge array of brass items from a $3 key chain to a $450 engine room telegraph from a ship. Although there is something for almost everyone's taste, many of the pieces have a nautical theme.

FORGET ME NOT SHOPPE (in the mall)

Forget Me Not Shoppe fans will find it on Main Street rather than Market Street. The theme is still country: wooden knickknacks, home decorations, wreaths, picture frames and the like. Ask them to show you the music boxes that play the theme from "Somewhere in Time."

Many store fronts received facelifts in the last few years.

BAG IT (in the mall)

Bags, bags, and more bags. Duffel bags, personalized bags, leather bags, nylon bags, fish net bags, backpacks. Anything you need to carry your fudge and more!

VILLAGE BLACKSMITH SHOP

Mackinac Island is known as the place where the horse is king, and the Village Blacksmith Shop pays homage to that king. You can have a souvenir horseshoe personalized with your name, or take home one of the many carousel horses or music boxes. Animal figurines are available in clay, glass, wood and pewter. In addition to the horse related items, the store also sells kites, kitchen knickknacks, toys, and ornaments.

PICTURE SHOP

A storehouse of memorable photos of Mackinac Island: old, new, black and white, color, framed, and unframed. Ask to browse through the boxes of unframed photos. They have everything, artfully photographed. A line of cards dominates one wall, and the rest of the shop features photo things, including place mats, books, and film.

3 SHIRTS TO THE WIND

A tiny shop with 29 different designs to choose from, including cartoon likenesses of Mackinac visitors. The shirts come in a variety of colors, including unusual tie-dyes.

RYBA'S FUDGE -- See page 90.

PROFESSOR HARRY'S OLD TIME PHOTOS

A new addition in 1989, Professor Harry's will dress you up in an old-time costume and take your picture. Professor Harry's is named after island businessman, Harry Ryba.

MICHELLE'S GIFTS

Michelle's is upstairs in the Orphan Corner Mall (by the Star Line Boat Dock). It carries a large selection of Mackinac island mugs, drink coolers, bags, T-shirts and other island souvenirs. It also has moccasins, stuffed animals, wooden boxes, hats and more hats.

DOCKSIDE T-SHIRT SHOP

Located dockside, next to the Star Line dock, this shop sells T-shirts of all kinds.

HIGHSTONE'S TOPSIDER

Highstone's carries T-shirts, sweatshirts, sweaters and a limited line of other clothing and, you guessed it, a line of footwear including Sperry Topsiders.

SCHWINN SHOP

This is the place for bicycle repairs, advice, and purchases. The Schwinn Shop sells new and used bicycles at good prices. And if you forgot to bring a lock for your own bicycle, you can get one here.

LAKESHORE GALLERY GIFTS

At the very end of town, Lakeshore Gallery Gifts carries nautical gifts, some leather products, film, and hats.

MARKET STREET SHOPPING DISTRICT

Market Street runs parallel to Main Street one block from the water. All of the shops are located between Astor Street and French Lane, on Market Street, or on one of the side streets connecting Market and Main. Listed beginning at the corner of Astor and Market, covering all of Market first, and then covering the side streets.

Market Street Shops
(shown in **bold** type)

French Lane

Hoban St. Cafe

The Landing Gull
Trafalgar Square
Town Crier office

Hart's Haven

Hoban Street

The Gallery
Village Inn

Heuer's Art Gallery *(in mall)*
Tassia's Gifts *(in mall)*
Le Galerie Dolls *(in mall)*
Pinnacle Shop *(in mall)*
Nadia's Fashions *(in mall)*
Grand Hotel in the Village
John S. Doud Gifts
Terwilliger's
First National Bank
Lilac Tree

Cloghaun

Metivier Inn

Biddle House

Benjamin Blacksmith Shop

Library

Astor Street Cafe
Mustang Lounge
Little Bob's
Pat's Boutique

City Hall & Police Department

American Fur Co. Warehouse (Community Hall)

Market Street

Astor Street

Arcade
Silver Mine

Stuart House

Post Office

walkway

Medical Center

Nadia's Fashions

Public rest rooms

Beaumont Memorial

Fort Street

```
┌─────────────────────────────────────────────────┐
│              Shops  on  Market  Street            │
└─────────────────────────────────────────────────┘
```

LILAC TREE

The Lilac Tree is the island's entry in discount clothing for both men and women. It also carries some island souvenirs and earrings.

TERWILLIGERS

A testament to the good taste and hobbies of the Terwilliger family of the East Bluff. Things horsey are featured with artifacts and pictures. But the wide range of treasures focuses on sailing, tennis, golf, and just pure enjoyment. Long-time summer residents, the owners have a shop that reflects their knowledge and enjoyment of the island.

JOHN S. DOUD GIFTS

For a view of how the island was "way back when," see John S. Doud's collection of old prints of the island. While you are there, pick up a T-shirt, sweatshirt, wooden toy, or ceramic sea gull.

GRAND HOTEL IN THE VILLAGE (Carousel Mall)

Like its sister store on Main Street, this Grand Hotel shop feels like the Grand Hotel. Its specialty is bath items, with an extensive line of soaps, oils, lotions, and potions. It also has handmade linens, including aprons, pillowcases, hand towels, and table runners. You can find a beautiful picture frame for your favorite island photograph, as well as unique Victorian birdhouses.

NADIA'S FASHION (Carousel Mall)

The junior-sized version of Nadia's on Fort Street (see page 87). Styles are younger and cater to the tastes of the summer employees. Sizes are 3 - 13.

PINNACLE SHOP (Carousel Mall)

One of the few shops selling fine jewelry, the Pinnacle offers items in both gold and sterling silver. It also has a selection of brass vases, lamps, and nautical merchandise.

LE GALERIE DOLLS AND MINIATURES (Carousel Mall)

A doll-lover's paradise, Le Galerie carries collectible dolls and miniatures and handmade teddy bears and gifts. Its main line is Madame Alexander collectible dolls, and it also has a large selection of porcelain dolls handmade by Michigan artists. A small selection of doll houses and doll house furniture is also available. Handmade Christmas ornaments (including island theme), music boxes, and children's books round out the offerings.

TASSIA'S GIFTS (Carousel Mall)

Tassia's features decorative items, including large pen drawings, watercolors of island scenes done in vivid colors by a local artist, and woven wall hangings. It also has a selection of cards, ornaments, sweaters, and costume jewelry.

HEUER'S WILDLIFE ART GALLERY (Carousel Mall)

Wildlife fans should have no trouble spending money at Heuer's. Wildlife art in many forms is available: decoys, prints, original paintings, posters, and other objects. Some of the art is created by the owner.

TRAFALGAR SQUARE

A world away from the fudge and souvenir shops, Trafalgar Square sells fine gift and decorative items in a distinguished atmosphere. Collectors' items include first edition books, original engravings by John James Audubon, music boxes, and lacquer boxes. Quilted and leather luggage and purses, English sweaters, perfumes, pipes, and Island note cards are included in the fine gift selection.

THE LANDING GULL

The sister store to the Landing Gull on Main Street, this store carries a similar selection of nautical gifts, Michigan artwork, and souvenirs.

Shops on Hoban Street, beginning at Market and Hoban

THE GALLERY

For those who have fallen in love with Mackinac during their stay, The Gallery is a great place to shop. It sells framed and unframed photography, watercolors, and pen and ink drawings of island and nature scenes. Over 75% of the works are done by Michigan artists. Most popular are the limited edition watercolor prints of Mackinac Island scenes. Also popular are rainy/foggy photographs of the island (that's when you really learn if you like it here) and floral prints, particularly of the island's adopted flower, the geranium.

---

*Shops on Astor Street, beginning
at the corner of Market and Astor*

PAT'S BOUTIQUE

Pat's Boutique has perfumes, cosmetics, inexpensive jewelry, vases, glassware, and souvenir items.

SILVER MINE

A gold mine of silver here on Astor Street. There are rings, bracelets, belt buckles, souvenir spoons, and earrings. If it's made in silver, you are likely to find it in this little yellow store.

Shops on Fort Street, beginning
at the corner of Market and Fort.

NADIA'S FASHIONS

Newly enlarged, Nadia's now boasts a ladies' section and a men's section. The overall theme is "coordinate, coordinate." Plain jackets match printed shorts that match printed sweaters. Budget to mid-priced.

The Fudge Factor

Return from a visit to Mackinac Island without some fudge for your friends, and you'll be in big trouble. Mackinac is known as the land of fudge. Day visitors are called fudgies and fudge is the island's only exported product. It all started in 1887 when the Murdick family saw the growth in Mackinac Island as a resort town, and jumped on the opportunity. They started selling fudge to satisfy Victorian sweet tooths, and the tradition was born. Now there are 13 individual fudge shops on the island, owned by six different owners, producing 33 different flavors!

As you stroll down Main Street, you can't help but smell the fudge. The secret recipes are mixed in huge copper kettles, heated, and then poured on to marble slabs to begin the cooling process. Then a fudge flipper begins creaming the fudge by walking around the table, flipping the mixture with a long-handled spatula. They can put on quite a show, trying to keep the fudge from falling on the floor! Finally, the fudge is worked into a loaf shape, and then sliced.

Fudge costs about $6.50 per pound (two slices). Senior citizen's discounts, where available, are 10% - 15%. Most of the stores will accept mail order requests between mid-May and mid-October.

I am often asked who makes the "best" fudge, but I don't know. When you grow up here, you quickly tire of fudge, so I don't have a favorite. But here's the lowdown on the locations (see map page 70), flavors, and policies of the fudge makers to help you in making this <u>very</u> important decision. ("FF" in the descriptions below indicates you can watch fudge being flipped at that location.)

The most popular souvenir of the island is fudge, handmade on marble slabs.

JoAnn's -- two stores, one on the west end of town, north side, next to Nephew's (FF) and the other in the center of town, south side, next to Benjamin's.   Flavors include: chocolate, chocolate pecan, chocolate walnut, chocolate almond, chocolate peanut butter, chocolate mint, chocolate cherry, vanilla pecan, maple pecan, butter pecan, peanut butter, rocky road, and penuche.   Peanut and cashew brittle, caramel corn, salt water taffy, and decorative tins also available.   Senior's discount.   Visa and Master Card accepted.

Kilwin's -- two stores, one next to the Arnold Line Dock in the center of town (FF) and another next to the Seasonal Shop on the west end of town, north side (FF).   Flavors include: German chocolate, chocolate English walnut, chocolate, chocolate pecan, chocolate black walnut, chocolate peanut butter, chocolate mint, vanilla pecan, butter pecan, maple walnut, rocky road, and peanut butter. A large selection of chocolates, dietetic chocolates, and hard candies available.   Ice cream, popcorn, caramel corn, salt water taffy, and decorative tins also available.   The store on the west end of town also carries brass and gift items.   Senior's discount.   Visa and Master Card accepted.

May's -- two stores in the middle of town, one on the north side at Astor Street, and the other on the south side, next to the Trading Post (FF).   Flavors include: chocolate pecan, chocolate, chocolate mint, vanilla pecan, butter pecan, maple pecan, rum, peanut butter, and natural black cherry.   Chocolates and brittle also available.   Senior's discount.   No credit cards accepted.

Murdick's -- three stores, one on the east end of town, north side, next to the Murray Hotel (FF), one in the middle of town, south side, next to Mr. B's (FF), and one in Surrey Hills.   Flavors include: chocolate pecan, chocolate, chocolate walnut, chocolate peanut butter, double chocolate, vanilla, vanilla pecan, Vermont maple pecan, butter pecan, peanut butter, and cranberry.   No credit cards accepted.

Murray -- one store, inside the Murray Hotel, north side of Main.   Flavors include: chocolate mint, chocolate, chocolate pecan, chocolate walnut, chocolate turtle, peanut butter chocolate, rocky road, vanilla walnut, vanilla pecan, vanilla, maple walnut, maple pecan, amaretto pecan, amaretto, amaretto walnut, amaretto turtle, peanut butter, and mint chocolate chip.   Gourmet jelly beans also available.   Visa and Master Card accepted.

Ryba's -- three stores, one on east end of town, south side, next to the Pancake House (FF), one in the middle of town,north side, next to the Scrimshaw Shop, and one near the Star Line dock on the west end of town (FF).   Flavors include: chocolate nut, chocolate no nut, vanilla nut, vanilla no nut, rum black walnut, coconut creme, strawberry, pistachio, maple, and peanut butter. Chocolates, chocolate covered Oreos and strawberries, peanut and cashew brittle, salt water taffy, and ice cream also available.   Senior's discount.   Visa and Master Card accepted.   Ryba's is the only year-round fudge operation. Ask them about their Christmas fudge packages.

GRAND HOTEL SHOPPING DISTRICT

Shoppers who are not guests of the hotel must pay a $5 admission fee to the hotel.   To get to the Grand, take Main Street to Hoban, turn right on Hoban to Market, turn left on Market and bear right around Chamber's Riding Stable. You are now on Cadotte, which you follow up the hill to the Grand.   The shops are all located on the lower level.

MACKINAC MARKET

The Mackinac Market is a larger version of the two Grand Hotel in the Village stores (Main Street and Market Street). It has a charming children's section of games, toys, and books.   Its book section is heavily weighted toward hardcover regional books, best sellers, and books on horses, decorating, yachting, and gardening.   This is the best spot to buy Grand Hotel memorabilia, including robes, bags, glasses, sweat shirts, posters, and hats.   And for those who want to pamper themselves or someone else, scented soaps, bubble bath and shampoos and creams are sold.

THE TOBACCONIST

The Tobacconist is the Grand's answer to a typical hotel gift shop, but even it isn't typical. It is the only place on the island where you can buy *The New York Times* (one day late, and be sure to call ahead to reserve a Sunday edition). In addition to the typical candy, cigarettes, aspirin, and other drug store items, the Tobacconist has magazines, paperbacks, and cards.

CARLETON'S TEA STORE

Named for Carleton Varney, the designer who did much of the decorating at the Grand, Carleton's is a combination sandwich and tea shop and gift store. It rates well as a limited menu restaurant (see page 66), and has excellent gifts for the culinary connoisseur. Carleton's has interesting cookbooks, homemade jams and jellies, key ingredients for south-of-the-border cooking, teas and coffees, and unusual pottery for the kitchen and dining room. And don't miss the fudge samples!

CAGNEY'S

Cagney's, "For the Man of the World," is a small upper-line clothing store for men. It also carries the "after six" Grand Hotel essentials -- sport coats, ties, and bow ties.

THE COLONY SHOP

The Colony Shop is a small upper-line clothing store for women, focusing primarily on casual wear. It also carries costume jewelry, lingerie, purses, and hats.

T. RICHARD'S

Tucked into a back corner on the lower level, T. Richard's is a destination the young and young at heart won't soon forget. Located right outside the arcade and craft room, T. Richard's has a wonderful collection of over 50 large glass canisters filled with treasures, candies, and trinkets. It also carries children's books, comic books, and coloring books.

OTHER LOCATIONS

VISITOR'S CENTER

Primarily designed as an information storehouse, the Visitor's Center also has a selection of island and regional publications, as well as some history theme souvenirs. The Visitor's Center is located across from Marquette Park.

SUTLER'S STORE - FORT MACKINAC

For some unusual gifts and mementos, check out the Sutler's Store. The most popular items are the period musical instruments, military hats, coloring books with historical themes, and regional publications.

ISLAND HOUSE GIFT SHOP

New in 1989, the Island House gift shop, located inside the Island House Hotel, carries toiletries, small gift items, and souvenirs.

MACKINAC MARINE SUPPLY

Just east of the marina in the Pub building, is the ultimate shop for sailors and for folks who like excellent gear. Classy sunglasses with famous names, foul weather clothing, and Patagonia jackets are all here. The other side of Hugh Ravitz's store gets practical and handles items to get yachters out of a jam, such as clips, hooks, line, and a full supply of nautical charts.

QUORUM ART GALLERY

If you are looking for an arty remembrance of your Mackinac trip, go to the Quorum Art Gallery at Mission Point Resort. The entrance is a little tricky to find (between the main building and the theater), but it is worth the effort. The Quorum displays artful works of all kinds -- ceramics, paintings, photography, and textiles -- created by northern Michigan artists.

MISSION POINT RESORT GIFT SHOP

The first of what is expected to be many shops at Mission Point, the gift shop carries higher end gifts, as well as toiletries and fine chocolates. Look for it across from the tennis courts.

Surrey Hills Shops

The Surrey Hills complex is at the top of the Grand Hotel Hill, past the Carriage Tour barns. Designed primarily as a transfer point between carriages during group carriage tours, Surrey Hill also has a number of shops.

LOON FEATHER

Like its sister store on Main Street, the Loon Feather at Surrey Hills carries Indian boxes, sweaters, stuffed animals, jewelry, and Hudson Bay woolens.

BALSAM SHOP

A smaller version of the Balsam Shop on Main Street, this store will keep your children busy looking through the treasures.

MACKINAC ISLAND PHOTOGRAPHY

If you want near-instant feedback on your photographic skills, drop your film off at Mackinac Island Photography and they'll have it back to you the same day. It also sells film and other photography supplies.

8
NATURAL ATTRACTIONS

You can view some of Mackinac Island's natural attractions before you arrive on the island. As you approach the harbor, you will see the high bluffs, the deep waters, and the luscious woods. You can begin to understand why Indians considered this land sacred and military leaders considered it a strategic post. It is because of the island's natural beauty and wealth that it developed into such an important historical location and tourist mecca.

After reviewing the island's natural attractions in general, I'll describe many of the sights in detail, and then wrap up with a suggested natural attractions tour. Remember as you explore the island not to disturb its beauty. Taking pictures is fine; taking mementos is illegal.

The Island's Formation

Geologists say that Mackinac became an island about 15,000 years ago, when the last glaciers receded from the area. The glaciers left a lake, later called "Algonquin." The highest part of the island, near what is now known as Fort

Holmes, was the only portion of the island visible above Lake Algonquin. The movement of Algonquin's waters created the island's bluffs and two of the limestone attractions, Skull Cave and Sugar Loaf.

About 9,000 years ago, Algonquin began to dry up. When it was at its lowest point, Mackinac Island and the two closest islands, Round and Bois Blanc, were connected to the mainland near the town of Cheboygan. Then the process reversed and, after another 4,000 years, one large lake called "Nippising" covered what are now Lakes Superior, Michigan, and Huron. Nippising's movements created more limestone formations, including Arch Rock, Friendship's Altar, and Eagle Point Cave. Over time, Nippising receded, leaving the three great lakes.

But the island's natural history has even deeper roots. The island's limestone formations began to form over 350 million years ago, when there was a thick layer of rock salt hundreds of feet below the area's limestone surface. As underground waters eroded the rock salt, large caverns were created below the surface. Over time, these collapsed, leaving stacks of broken limestone. Water gradually cemented these pieces together. Then Algonquin and Nippising washed away the softer rock around the stacks, leaving formations similar to what we see today. This type of formation, made of broken and re-cemented limestone, is called *brecciated* limestone, and is unique to northern Michigan.

The Surrounding Waters

Mackinac Island sits in Lake Huron, near the Straits of Mackinac, which is a 50-mile passage connecting Lake Huron and Lake Michigan. Lake Huron has a surface area of 23,000 miles and is over 600 feet deep in some places. The Straits are an important shipping channel, with freighters carrying iron ore, coal, and lumber through its waters daily.

The area's waters are teeming with fish. The local favorite is whitefish, and you'll notice it on many of the island menus. Lake trout, once nearly depleted due to the invasion of parasitic sea lamprey, are again prevalent thanks to a program of regulatory controls and restocking. Salmon are also becoming a favorite among the sporting fisherman. See Chapter Ten for information on fishing trips.

Living Things

Mackinac Island's unique weather and soil conditions put it in a transition zone for plant life between the softwood and evergreen (conifer) forests of the north and the mixed hardwoods of the south. The result is a bounty for nature lovers, with a wide variety of trees and wild flowers.

The island's trees include the conifers -- balsam, cedar, spruce, tamarack -- and the hardwoods -- beech, black locust, red oak, and sugar maple. The South Bicycle Trail is an excellent place to view the varieties, as they are well marked along this route.

The island's wild flowers number over 400 species, spread throughout a range of habitats. Walk slowly along any of the island's trails and you are sure to be pleased by the delicate flowers.

Along the *beaches*, look for beach pea, wrinkled rose, silverweed and sedum; in the *bogs,* look for blueberries, heath, and wild orchids; in the *marshes* look for marsh marigold, March blue violet, cattails, and mints; in the *meadows* look for daisies, wild strawberries, blue-eyed grass and campions; in the *softwood forests* look for bead lily, calypso orchid and twin flower; and in the *hardwood forests* look for trillium, mayflower and trout lily.

The island's wildlife is not as varied as its plant life. Mackinac's year-round bird population is primarily purple finch, red-breasted nuthatch, and black-capped chickadee. The summer population swells with the addition of herring and ring-billed sea gulls, robins, yellow warblers, chimney swifts, American redstart, ovenbirds, and a variety of swallows. The most prominent mammals (of the wild variety) are red and grey squirrels, bats, raccoons, chipmunks, and rabbits.

Arch Rock is a spectacular limestone bridge.

Sights to See

ANNE'S TABLET

My favorite getaway on Mackinac Island is Anne's Tablet on the bluff just east of Fort Mackinac. It is a memorial to Constance Fenimore Woolson, an author who wrote of the island's beauty in the late 1800's. It is a wonderful place for quiet reflection, with myrtle-covered hills and a harbor view. I hesitate to "give away" the directions, but take Crow's Nest Trail (behind the playground at Marquette Park) up the hill, and follow the path to your left along the bluff.

ARCH ROCK

Arch Rock, located on the island's eastern shore, is the most spectacular of the island's brecciated limestone formations. The limestone arch rises 146 feet above the water and spans fifty feet. There is a stairway from the Lake Shore Road up to the top of the arch.

Indian legend says the arch was formed when an Indian maiden, forbidden by her father to marry the warrior of her dreams, cried for so long and with such intensity that her tears washed away the bluff's stone and created the arch. The sad story has a happy ending; the warrior appears and takes the maiden with him to his home among the sky people. The Indians also believed that Arch Rock was where the Great Spirit entered the island before taking up residence in Sugar Loaf, the great wigwam.

SUGAR LOAF

Sugar Loaf, the largest of the island's limestone stacks, towers 75 feet above the ground. Lake Algonquin once covered Sugar Loaf up to the point of the small cave on the stack's north side. You can find Sugar Loaf by following Sugar Loaf Road.

SKULL CAVE

Skull Cave is one of the island's oldest formations, and has an interesting history. The cave was formed as Lake Algonquin's waves washed against a large limestone stack and eroded a portion of its western side, leaving a cave. The cave was apparently used as an Indian burial ground, as Alexander Henry, a British merchant, discovered. He hid there one night after the Indians took Fort Michilimackinac on the mainland in 1763, and when he woke, discovered the bones. Skull Cave is at the intersection of Garrison and Rifle Range Roads.

CAVE IN THE WOODS

Cave in the Woods is a small cave located near the island's airport. It was created about 10,000 years ago, when the location was a beach of Lake Algonquin.

CRACK IN THE ISLAND

Near Cave in the Woods is Crack in the Island, a long shallow fissure in the surface limestone. This crack was formed in much the same way as the limestone formations, as water eroded the softer rock and left brecciated limestone.

DEVIL'S KITCHEN

Located on Mackinac's western shore, Devil's Kitchen is one of the youngest limestone formations on the island. Although the limestone has been in place for over 350 million years, the erosion forming the small cave has taken place in the last few centuries.

" My favorite thing to do on Mackinac Island is to ride around the shore road, and to walk in the woods near Arch Rock and the Leslie Avenue area.

To get to know the island, you must spend more than a day, and see more than the downtown area. A carriage or bike tour is a good introduction, and then you should explore to really appreciate the beauty of the island. I think Mackinac Island's beauty and uniqueness stands out from any place in Michigan and perhaps the United States."

Margaret Doud,
Mayor of Mackinac Island

BROWN'S BROOK

Brown's Brook is a beautiful spot on the island's eastern shore. It is fed by an underground spring and flows year-round.

CROGHAN WATER

Croghan Water is a seasonal marsh near British Landing. In the spring, it is an excellent spot to see vegetation and animals. It is named after Colonel Croghan who lead the American troops in the ill-fated attempt to regain Fort Mackinac from the British in July of 1814.

Natural Attractions Tour

It is difficult to go anywhere on Mackinac Island without seeing its natural beauty. But if you are really interested in exploring its natural side, you need to go up into the middle of the island. I've designed a tour that will get you to most of the more impressive sites. Because of the distances involved, you should go on a bicycle. Even on a bicycle, the tour is fairly rigorous and will take you about three hours.

Beginning at the western edge of Marquette Park, push your bike up Fort Street, through the brown gates, and up the hill. Turn right at the Governor's summer residence, and go past the back of Fort Mackinac. Go across the main intersection and pick up the South Bicycle Trail (there's a sign with a bicycle on it). The Mackinac Island State Park Commission has done an excellent job of identifying trees along this trail. Take it to Arch Rock.

After viewing Arch Rock, take Rifle Range Road (to your right when your back is to Arch Rock) to its end, and turn right on Garrison Road. Explore Skull Cave, and then take Garrison Road past the cemeteries, and turn right on Fort Holmes Road. To your left is a hardwood forest. Stay to the right, and go up to Fort Holmes (the highest point on the island) for a fantastic view of the entire Straits area.

Congratulate yourself, because it's all down hill from Fort Holmes. On the way down, bear to the right, and look out over Sugar Loaf. Take Fort Holmes Road back to Garrison Road and turn right.

Follow Garrison past the end of the air strip and past the intersection of four roads, (where Garrison turns into British Landing Road), and turn left on State Road. Park and lock your bikes, and hike on the trail to your left to examine Cave of the Woods and Crack in the Island.

Take State Road back to British Landing Road and turn left. Take British Landing Road past the battlefield meadow on your right, and the marshes of Croghan Water. Stop in the nature center at British Landing where the attendant can answer any questions you may have.

Turn right on the shore road, and on the way back to town, stop at the Wild Flower Trail and exhibits, and view Arch Rock from the shore.

A sacred place for early Indians, Sugar Loaf continues to amaze visitors.

9
HISTORICAL TREASURES

The Straits area is a history lover's delight. Along these picturesque shores, Indians, French Jesuits, British fur traders and American soldiers lived, worked, and played. Later, Victorian travelers discovered the island's treasures. Through the efforts of the Mackinac Island State Park Commission, the City of Mackinac Island, and the chambers of commerce of Mackinac Island, Mackinaw City and St. Ignace, this rich history comes alive for the inquisitive modern-day visitor.

The best way to learn about the island's history is to visit the historical attractions, view the displays, and talk to the well-informed guides. Then wander through the attractions and picture for yourself what has transpired on this island in the last 300 years.

To help set the stage for your visits to the historical attractions, I'll provide a "short course" in island history, and then review each attraction in detail. At the end, I'll recommend some routes for you to take on your historical exploration and some side trips to historical treasures in the Straits area near the island.

"Short Course" in
Mackinac Island History

The first records of Mackinac Island history are found in Indian lore, which says that the island appeared one day out of a deep fog that had clouded the Straits for several days. The Indian meaning of the name is still disputed, but most accounts indicate that Michilimackinac (later shortened to Mackinac) means the great turtle, referring the the island's shape. The other theory is that the Indian name for the island was actually Mishi-min-auk-in-ong, which meant place of the great dancing spirits. The Indians believed that the Great Spirit came to the island to live among his people in the large limestone wigwam (Sugar Loaf). The island served as a sacred land for many Indians, and they offered gifts to the spirits on the island and buried their dead throughout its woods.

Almost all the Indians in the area were descendants of the Algonquin, Iroquois or Sioux tribes. The tribes frequently had conflicts among themselves, but the arrival of the French intensified the struggle. The land was rich with natural resources and, for the Indians, it was sacred. For the non-Indians, it represented a strategic location.

The first non-Indian reported to have traveled through the Straits was Jean Nicolet. Nicolet was a French explorer en route from Quebec to what he believed was China in 1664 when he traveled through the Straits, discovered Wisconsin, and almost reached the Mississippi River. In 1669, Father Jean Claude Allouez, a French Jesuit, visited the island from his mission at Sault Ste. Marie. That same year, Father Claude Dablon built a bark chapel on the island to help spread Christianity among Indians of the Straits area. Because of the isolation of the island in the winter, Dablon decided to re-establish the mission on the mainland near what is now St. Ignace, and directed Father Jacques Marquette to lead this mission.

Father Marquette was a key figure
in the area's history.

Meanwhile, interest was building among the French to explore what Nicolet had called the "Great Water" (the Mississippi, which he believed was the ocean). Louis Joliet and Father Marquette were sent in 1674 to find the Great Water, and they did.

The Jesuits were great explorers, but their amicable relationships with the Indians were increasingly at odds with French economic and military desires. The importance of spreading Christianity became secondary to the importance of expanding the fur trade; the Jesuits received less support, and by the mid-1700's, had little influence in the area.

Fur pelts were rapidly becoming the currency of the day, and the French wanted to establish a series of fur trading posts, linked with forts, throughout the Great Lakes. Toward this end, they built Fort de Baude in 1690 in St. Ignace, near where the Jesuits had established their mission. The Fort operated for about 10 years before it was ordered closed and the operations moved to Fort Pontchartrain (Detroit).

The French move opened the way for the British to establish a presence in the Straits. When the French realized their mistake, they returned to the area, and in 1715 constructed Fort Michilimackinac (Mackinaw City). In the ensuing years, the French and the British continued to skirmish. When the skirmishes turned to war, the British won Canada, which encompassed much of the Midwest, including Michigan.

The British did not cultivate relationships with the Indians as the French had, and consequently had disastrous results. In 1763, what looked like an Indian game during celebrations of King George's birthday turned into an Indian capture of Fort Michilimackinac and a massacre of British soldiers. Fearing British retaliation, the Indians moved to a more defensible position on Mackinac Island. When they didn't get the support they expected from the French, the Indians ended their stand, and the British moved back to Fort Michilimackinac within the year. But the British had learned the importance of developing rapport with local Indian tribes.

When the British at Michilimackinac learned of the American Revolution, they decided, as the Indians had in 1763, that they should move to a more defensible position on Mackinac Island. Major Patrick Sinclair and his troops began moving buildings and supplies across the ice in the winter of 1779-80. By that summer, the move was complete. A fortress was built on the bluff overlooking the harbor, while settlers and traders built homes along the shore. Despite continued rumors that the Americans were going to attack the fort, there were no British-American battles at the Straits during the Revolution. The area was transferred to the Americans in the Treaty of Paris in 1783, but the British managed to delay turning Fort Mackinac over to the Americans until 1796.

In the early 1800's, the Americans worked to establish dominance in the fur trade, but their plans were upset in 1812 when the U.S. Government declared war against the British.   The new government's communication system was poor, and the Americans on Mackinac Island did not learn of the war until the British secretly landed on the back of the island (British Landing), hauled a cannon up to its highest point (Fort Holmes), and pointed it down at Fort Mackinac.   The Americans surrendered Fort Mackinac without a shot, and the British were back in command.

The Americans tried to recapture the island in 1814, using the strategy of approaching from British Landing.   But the British were prepared for the attack, and after a bloody battle, the Americans retreated.   Not long afterward, they attempted a naval blockade of the island, but that failed too.

Mackinac Island was returned to the Americans through the Treaty of Ghent, signed in 1814.   Because the U. S. Government prohibited British companies from doing business in the United States, the Americans quickly took the lead in the fur trading industry.   John Jacob Astor consolidated his hold, setting up headquarters of his American Fur Trading Company on Mackinac Island.   In time, he became extremely prosperous and was one of the country's first millionaires.   Fur trading remained the dominant force on the island until the 1840's, when a decline in demand and a reduced supply of pelts combined to hurt the business.

The decline in the fur trade caused Mackinac Island merchants to look for a new industry.   They realized what the Indians had known for years -- that the Straits were filled with fish.   The island quickly transformed from a fur trading to a fishing base.

Fishing shanties, processing shops, and related businesses popped up on Main Street.   Several docks were built.   The fishermen used nets to catch the fish, and then brought them to Mackinac Island to be processed and shipped by steamship to Detroit, Chicago, and other major markets. Mackinac's economy was dependent on fishing for about

40 years, until a combination of over-fishing and increased tourism caused another dramatic shift in the island's industry about 1880.

At that time, the steamship and railroad companies were looking for passengers and began to promote Mackinac Island as an idyllic summer getaway for upper middle-class Midwesterners. By the 1870's, several hotels were in operation. In 1875, Congress named much of Mackinac Island the nation's second national park (after Yellowstone), securing its future as a tourist mecca.

The industrialization of America was creating a leisure class that wanted to escape the heat and pollution of the cities in the summer. They expected to travel in luxury, and the steamship and railroad companies were happy to oblige. The first railroad reached Mackinaw City in 1881, and regular ferry service to the island began that same year. The island put on a new set of clothes, changing out of its fishing garb into a wardrobe a Victorian socialite

Many of the early summer residents were from Chicago.

would enjoy: fashionable shops, excellent restaurants, and increasingly sophisticated hotels. Travellers would arrive on the docks accompanied by maids and servants, and equipped with trunks filled with elaborate clothing for the events of the day -- formal meals, teas, and dances. Many would stay for the entire summer.

Demand quickly grew for private cottages. Gurdon Hubbard, who had worked for the American Fur Trading Company and then made and lost his fortune in Chicago, decided to develop his 80 acres of land on the island. He sold his first lots in 1882, and Charles Caskey, a builder from Harbor Springs, quickly built several cottages in Hubbard's Annex. The national park then began leasing land to prospective cottage owners, and building began on the island's eastern and western bluffs. Proceeds from these leases were used to improve the park properties.

Many of the original cottages were much simpler than you see today, as they were expanded as the island gained favor as a summer resort. The building boom continued; by the mid-1890's, cottages were built on most of the lots in the East and West Bluffs, and Hubbard's Annex.

In 1887, a consortium of railroad and steamship companies hired Charles Caskey to build a showplace hotel on a hill overlooking the Straits. It was a gamble designed to increase traffic on the railroads and steamships headed for the island. The original portion of the Grand Hotel was built in four months, almost exclusively of Michigan white pine. It was a struggle to keep the 200 rooms full, and the short eight week season made it difficult to break even.

But by the turn of the century, thanks to aggressive promotional activity, the Grand was on its way to success. This gamble by the consortium firmly established Mackinac Island as a resort town.

Two other key decisions were made around the turn of the century that improved Mackinac's position as a resort. In 1895, the U.S. Government transferred its properties on the island to the State of Michigan, making it the state's first state park. This move ensured that the island would be protected from developers seeking to expand the residential and commercial building on the island. And in 1896, the first actions were taken to prohibit motor vehicles from operating on the island.

Throughout the 1900's, the island solidified its position as a major destination for travelers in the Midwest. More

The Arnold Line dock was as busy in 1910 as it is today, and much more orderly!

hotels and businesses opened, and the state began to improve its land and facilities as tourist attractions. In the 1920's, the state doubled the size of the park, and eventually over 80% of the island became a state park. The old fort pasture was turned into a visitor park, and other historical buildings -- including the Indian Dormitory and the Biddle House -- were acquired by the state. The island weathered the depression and two world wars fairly well. Tourism received a boost when the Mackinac Bridge was completed in 1957, connecting Michigan's upper and lower peninsulas. Not long afterwards, the state began an aggressive program of excavation and renovation beginning with Fort Mackinac.

Overview of Historical Attractions

Before setting out on your history tour, read the attraction descriptions below and decide which you want to see. I'll include some suggested routes at the end of the chapter, but your interests will determine a route appropriate for you.

Most of the attractions require an Historic Mackinac Ticket, which can be purchased at the State Park Kiosk in Marquette Park, Visitor's Center (just across from Marquette Park next to the Chippewa Hotel), or Fort Mackinac. Tickets are $5.50 for adults (13 and over), and $2.75 for children (ages 6 - 12). Family passes are available for $16.50 (2 adults and their dependent children). If you plan to visit Fort Michilimackinac, the Welcome, and Old Mill Creek (all in Mackinaw City), which I recommend if you have time, buy a combination ticket that includes those attractions. The Mackinac Combination Ticket is $10.00 for adults and $5.00 for children.

VISITOR'S CENTER

The Visitor's Center, located across from Marquette Park and next to the Chippewa Hotel, is an excellent place to get information about the island. They sell a wide range of publications about the island, and have informative displays and staff ready to answer your questions.

INDIAN DORMITORY

Just east of Marquette Park, the Indian Dormitory has been turned into a museum by the Mackinac Island State Park Commission. Admission is by Historic Mackinac Island Ticket.

Although it was not built until 1838, after the Indians sold their rights to the island land in exchange for financial and humanitarian assistance in the Treaty of Washington, the Indian Dormitory is the best place on the island to get a sense of Indian history. It contains a wealth of information about Henry Schoolcraft, the Indian agent at Mackinac in the 1830's who, in addition to his formal duties, studied the Indians in great detail. His account is one of the best references on 18th and 19th century Indian life. The Indian Dormitory also contains numerous Indian artifacts and dioramas arranged along the theme of Henry Wadsworth Longfellow's classic poem, *Hiawatha*. Longfellow was a friend of Schoolcraft's, and based his poem on Schoolcraft's works.

FORT MACKINAC

Located on the bluff high above the harbor, Fort Mackinac is a must for island visitors. Admission is by Historic Mackinac Ticket and there are two entrances: one up the ramp above Marquette Park (it's a tough climb, but benches are provided), and the other at the Avenue of Flags on Huron Road just past the Governor's summer residence.

You'll immediately see why the British chose this site, with its commanding view of the Straits, for their fort. Start your tour with the short slide presentation shown regularly in the Commissary Building near the main entrance. After that, tour the buildings in any order you like, and make sure to watch the musket and cannon firing exhibitions. You'll find that each building has a self-contained story, and that many interpreters are available to answer your questions.

College students in military costume fire cannons from Fort Mackinac daily.

BRITISH LANDING

British Landing is on the far side of the island, and is where the British landed in 1812 to launch their surprise attack on the Americans at Fort Mackinac. There is little to see at the spot now, except a beautiful view of the water and Michigan's upper peninsula. There are public rest rooms, a snack shop, and a nature center with an attendant to answer your questions.

BATTLEFIELD OF 1814

Up British Landing Road from British Landing is the Battlefield of 1814. This time it was the Americans landing at British Landing in an attempt to regain Fort Mackinac. After a bloody battle on this site, the Americans retreated.

FORT HOLMES

A visit to Fort Holmes on the island's highest point requires you to expend some energy, but the view is worth the effort. This is where the British surprised the Americans at Fort Mackinac during the War of 1812. They dragged their cannon from the back of the island (British Landing) during the night, pointed them down at Fort Mackinac, and forced the Americans to surrender without a shot.

The site was fortified with a small stockade and blockhouse, and all that remains is a reconstruction of the stockade... and a spectacular view of the Straits. The Fort is 168 feet above Fort Mackinac and 325 feet above the Straits.

GOVERNOR'S SUMMER RESIDENCE

The Governor's summer residence is owned by the State of Michigan, and is just to the west of Fort Mackinac on the bluff. It was built in 1902 for a prominent Chicago attorney at a cost of $15,000. The state purchased the 24-room home in 1945, and it serves as a summer house for the state's governor. If the Michigan flag is flying outside, the Governor is in residence. The gazebo in the yard was used in the movie "*Somewhere In Time*." The first floor of the home is open for public tours on Wednesdays from 9:30 - 11:30 a.m. Just stop by the house; admission is free.

Michigan's governors have a history of falling in love with the island while in office. Former Governors G. Mennen Williams and William Milliken both moved out of the Governor's summer residence and into their own summer house on the island.

"*The uniqueness of Mackinac Island is its people and its history. It is a living history book. The names of many persons living on the island the year around -- French, Indian, early missionaries and pioneers -- carry with them the events of three centuries ago. Those events are memorialized for visitors in the artistic exhibits, some life-size, at Fort Mackinac, sponsored by the Mackinac Island State Park Commission.*

Visitors start coming to the island in May with the opening of its season. As the season moves on, nearly one million citizens, hundreds of whom come season after season, will visit. The bicyclists are a happy lot, taking in the view of the island's setting in the Great Lakes around a virtually level paved highway. The island is a recreational retreat from homes where the automobile is king because of a declaration that here the horse is king."

> Wesley H. Maurer, Sr., Co-Editor and Co-Publisher
> *Mackinac Island Town Crier* and *St. Ignace News*
> Professor Emeritus, University of Michigan.

Market Street Area

(Listed in order as you walk from the corner of Market and Fort Streets away from Marquette Park.)

McGULPIN HOUSE

McGulpin House is one of the oldest structures on the island, dating back to around 1780. It is located near the corner of Market and Fort Streets, and admission is by Historic Mackinac Ticket. It has been restored to the 1780's era, and includes an exhibit showing the construction techniques of the time.

BEAUMONT MEMORIAL

On the corner of Market Street and Fort Street, the Beaumont Memorial is a tribute to Dr. William Beaumont,

an Army physician at the Fort.   Admission is by Historic
Mackinac Ticket.

In 1882, Alexis St. Martin, a young man shopping in the
American Fur Trading Company store, was accidentally
shot in the stomach.   Dr. Beaumont treated him, but the
hole in his stomach would not heal.   Beaumont was able to
conduct numerous experiments by lowering foods into St.
Martin's stomach through the hole, and eventually made
significant discoveries as to how the human digestive
system works.   The Memorial includes dioramas of
Beaumont and St. Martin.

MATHEW GEARY HOUSE (not open to the public)

When you leave the Beaumont Memorial, walk by the
Mathew Geary House next door.   It was built sometime
before 1848, and is typical of mid-19th century
architecture on the island.

ROBERT STUART HOUSE

Located just east of Astor on Market Street, the Robert
Stuart House is a museum operated by the City of Mackinac
Island.   Admission is $1.00 for adults and $.50 for children.

From 1817 to 1837 this was the home of Robert Stuart, the
manager of the American Fur Trading Company on
Mackinac Island.   In the 1840's, it served as the island's
first hotel.   Now it is chock full of antiques, artifacts,
memorabilia, sketches and photographs of the island and
its inhabitants.   Take your time wandering through the
rooms, and ask the staff questions -- they have great
stories to tell!

AMERICAN FUR COMPANY WAREHOUSE

Next to the Robert Stuart House, the American Fur
Company Warehouse is where fur pelts were sorted,
graded, cleaned and pressed for shipment east.   Built in
1810, it now serves as the island's community hall.

COUNTY COURTHOUSE

From 1834, when it was built, until 1882, the next building served as the county court house. Now it houses the police, jail, and city council chambers.

EDWARD BIDDLE HOUSE

The Edward Biddle House is located on Market Street between Astor and Hoban Streets, and admission is by Historic Mackinac Ticket.

This house is one of the oldest structures downtown, originally built as early as 1780. It is restored and furnished as it was when Edward Biddle, a prominent and prosperous fur trader, lived there. Interpreters demonstrate wool spinning and baking.

BENJAMIN BLACKSMITH SHOP

Behind the Biddle House, the Benjamin Blacksmith Shop is a working museum that is guaranteed to delight the children in your crowd. Watch the smithy continue in the tradition of long-time island blacksmith Herbert Benjamin, as he coaxes iron into wagon rims, street light brackets and candle holders, some of which are available for sale. Admission is by Historic Mackinac Ticket.

Steeple Chase

LITTLE STONE CHURCH

Located at the bottom of the Grand Hill on Cadotte Avenue is the Little Stone Congregational Church, with its stained glass windows depicting scenes from the island's history. The congregation was formed in 1896 and the church was completed in 1904. The building is open to the public when services are not being held. The church is open only in the summer.

MISSIONARY BARK CHAPEL

The Bark Chapel, in Marquette Park near the corner of Market and Fort Streets, is similar to what Father Claude Dablon constructed on the island in 1669. Inside you can see exhibits about Father Dablon's mission.

TRINITY EPISCOPAL CHURCH

Across from the Bark Chapel is Trinity Episcopal Church, which was built in 1882. Episcopalian services were held on the island beginning in 1842, and a congregation was formed in 1873. The building is open to the public when services are not being held.

ST. ANNE'S CATHOLIC CHURCH

St. Anne's is located on Huron Street at Church Street, two blocks east of Marquette Park. Although the current building was built in 1878, the Catholic roots on the island go back to Father Dablon in the mid-1600's. The first St. Anne's church was at Fort Michilimackinac in Mackinaw City, and it was one of the first buildings moved across the ice to the island when the British moved the fort. The original island site was on Hoban Street where the Michigan Bell building is today.

There is a museum in the basement of the church that includes records, articles, and paintings from the original church. The building is open to the public when services are not being held. St. Anne's is the only church that is open year-round and so it enjoys a large local attendance.

MISSION CHURCH

Mission Church, located on Huron Street just west of Mission Point Resort, is the oldest surviving church building in Michigan. It was built in 1829, in New England style architecture. It was recently purchased and renovated by the Mackinac Island State Park Commission.

Suggested Historical Routes

After you've read about the historical attractions, pick out the ones you'd like to see, and plot your own route using the map on page 14.   For those who want to pick a "standard" tour, three possibilities are outlined below.

Tour One: Early Indian and Military History
        (about 2 1/2 hours)

Beginning at Marquette Park, stop at the Visitor's Center or the State Park Kiosk and buy a Mackinac Island Historic ticket.   Then explore the Bark Chapel and the Father Marquette memorial.   Wander over to the Indian Dormitory and learn more about Indian life.   On your way up the hill to Fort Mackinac, stop at the McGulpin House to see how the early settlers lived.   Then explore Fort Mackinac, learning about its military history.   Exit the fort at the Avenue of Flags, turn left, and see the Governor's summer residence straight ahead.   Bear left at the Governor's, and return to Marquette Park.

Tour Two: Fur Traders, Tourist Trade,
        and Victorian Cottages
        (about 3 hours)

Beginning at the west end of Marquette Park, take Fort Street one block north (away from the lake) to Market Street and turn left.   With your Historic Mackinac Ticket, explore the buildings on Market Street and learn about the exploits of Beaumont, Astor, Stuart (additional charge), Biddle and Benjamin.   Continue on Market Street until you reach the Chamber's Riding Stable, where you turn right on Cadotte Avenue, and follow it up to the Grand Hotel.   Pay the $5/person admission fee and explore the Grand.   Leave the main entrance of the Grand and turn right.   Take this road (West Bluff) past the cottages on the west bluff.   Most of these are in the Queen Anne Victorian style and were built in the late 1800's.   The fourth one past the Grand is the former home of the late Governor G. Mennen Williams.

Bear right and then take your first left. Take your next left onto an unpaved road. Follow this road until you reach the large, white, columned Greek Revival home on your left. Turn right and go through Hubbard's Annex (see page 108). Then turn right again at the main road (Annex Road) and follow this back to the Carriage Tour Barns, bear right, and go down the Grand Hotel Hill (Cadotte Avenue). Turn left at the Chamber's Riding Stable and follow Market Street back to Marquette Park.

Built in the 1890's, this cottage on the West Bluff is an example of Queen Anne architecture.

Tour Three: Forts and Battlefields
(about two hours)

Bicycles are recommended for this tour, which will take you past the island's forts and battlefields. Beginning at Marquette Park, push your bike up the street bordering the park (Fort Street), through the brown gates and to the Governor's summer residence. Turn right, and ride past (or if you have time, stop and visit) Fort Mackinac. Turn left on the first main road (Garrison). Go past Skull Cave (see page 98) and the cemeteries. Turn right just past the second cemetery on your right (Fort Holmes Road). Bear right on Fort Holmes Road and take to the end and explore Fort Holmes. If you've brought a picnic, this is the place to enjoy it. On your way back down Fort Holmes Road, bear right, and enjoy the lookout over Sugar Loaf (see page 98). When you get back to the cemetery, turn right on Garrison Road. Take this to the main intersection, where it turns into British Landing Road. Follow British Landing Road past the Battlefield of 1814 and Croghan Water, and to British Landing. Explore British Landing, and then take the shore road left or right back to town (left is shorter).

Related Historical Outings

If you enjoy history, try to make time in your travel plans to visit some of the following:

FORT MICHILIMACKINAC
616/436-5563
Fort Michilimackinac in Mackinaw City is a reconstruction of the fur-trading village and fort established in 1715 by the French on that site. There are ongoing archaeological digs, craft demonstrations, costumed guides, and displays for visitors to enjoy. There is also a maritime museum inside the restored 1892 Mackinac Point Lighthouse on the site. Admission includes Fort Michilimackinac, the Maritime Museum, and the Welcome (see below) and is $5.50 for adults and $2.75 for children (ages 6 - 12). Admission is also by Mackinac Combination Ticket (see page 110).

MACKINAC BRIDGE MUSEUM
616/436-5534
A former ironworker developed this museum above his pizzeria in Mackinaw City to recognize the people who built the Mackinac Bridge. It contains interesting tools and artifacts, and a continuously running film about the bridge's construction. Admission is free. The museum is located above Mama Mia's Pizza in Mackinaw City.

TEYSEN'S WOODLAND INDIAN MUSEUM
616/436-7011
Above Teysen's Restaurant in Mackinaw City is a museum well worth the trip. It includes Indian artifacts, information about the natural history of the Straits area, and displays depicting the region's maritime history. Admission is $1.00 for adults and $.50 for children.

The British used the sloop Welcome to move buildings across the Straits from Fort Michilimackinac to Fort Mackinac.

THE WELCOME
616/436-5563
The Revolutionary War Sloop Welcome, docked at the Mackinaw City Marina, is a reconstructed 1775 British sloop that sailed the Great Lakes during the American Revolution. Visitors can relive the maritime history of the area while exploring the vessel. Admission is $1.50 for adults and $.75 for children (and included in Fort Michilimackinac or Mackinac Combination Tickets).

OLD MILL CREEK
616/436-7301
Old Mill Creek is a 625-acre park on U.S. 23 just outside Mackinaw City. Its main attraction is a working reconstructed 18th century watermill. Enjoy craft demonstrations, nature trails, a multi-media orientation program, and a picnic area. Admission is $3.00 for adults and $1.50 for children (ages 6 - 12). Admission is also available through the Mackinac Combination Ticket.

MUSEUM OF OJIBWA CULTURE
906/436-5534
This museum, in downtown St. Ignace tells the story of Ojibwa (also known as Chippewa) life in the Straits area. It is built on the site of the Father Marquette mission, and archaeological digs continue to uncover artifacts from that era. The museum is open daily from Memorial Day through mid-October. Admission is $1.00 for adults and $.50 for children, or $3.00 for a family.

SAULT STE. MARIE BOAT LOCKS

The "Soo" is one of Michigan's oldest cities and home to the Soo locks, connecting Lakes Superior and Huron. It is a 55-mile drive from St. Ignace. For additional information, contact the Sault Area Chamber of Commerce: 2581 I-75 Business Spur, Sault Ste. Marie, MI 49783, 906/632-3301.

10
GOOD SPORTS

With clean air and beautiful scenery, Mackinac Island is a natural for sports enthusiasts. The options are many and, in most cases, the costs are minimal.

The suggested routes for bicycling, hiking and jogging described below are designed for both exercising and sightseeing. They are organized from easiest to most difficult by category. You are also encouraged to create your own routes; if you get lost, you will eventually find the water and your way home! Because there are so few directional signs, I've tried where possible to include landmarks in the directions.

If you are looking for walking tours of the natural or historical attractions, see chapters Eight or Nine.

BICYLING

Bicycles are an excellent way to explore the island while getting exercise. (See Chapter Five for information on bringing your own bicycle or renting one on the island.)

Chapter Five also describes areas where you should not take your bike, and some rules of the road. See the map on page 14 to design your route, or take one of my favorites:

'Round the Rock -- 8.2 miles of the most level ground you'll find on Mackinac Island. Take Main Street from town in either direction and follow the paved road along the water all the way around the island. You'll see beautiful water, two limestone formations (Arch Rock and Devil's Kitchen), British Landing, and the Wild Flower Trail.

South Bicycle Trail Saunter -- approximately four miles on paved roads with several key sights and only one large uphill stretch. From Marquette Park, take Main Street east (away from town). Turn left on Mission Street, which is just past Haan Cottage. Ride or push your bike up Mission Hill (most push!). Stay to the left at the top of the hill and take Huron Street past the East Bluff cottages.

Turn right on the South Bicycle Trail (at the intersection of three paved roads, and marked with a bicycle sign) and follow it to Arch Rock. Take Rifle Range Road (to your right when your back is to Arch Rock) to Sugar Loaf Road and turn right. Sugar Loaf Road loops past Sugar Loaf and then ends back at Rifle Range Road. Turn right on Rifle Range Road and follow it until it ends at Garrison Road, where you turn left. Turn right on Huron (the first road to the right) and go past Fort Mackinac. Turn left on Fort Street (Governor's summer residence is straight ahead). Walk your bike down Fort Street.

North Bicycle Trail Trek -- approximately six miles, fairly hilly, mostly paved. From Marquette Park, take Fort Street (bordering west end of Park) up the hill (you'll need to push your bike between the gates). Go past the Governor's summer residence and turn right and pass Fort Mackinac. Turn left on Garrison Road, pass the South Bicycle Trail and take a right on the North Bicycle Trail. As you approach the large paved road (Rifle Range) veer left on to a short path. Cross Rifle Range Road and continue on the wide asphalt and dirt path.

Pass Sugar Loaf on your right and the stairs to Point Lookout on your left, and continue on the North Bicycle Trail until it ends at Leslie Avenue. Turn left down the hill onto Leslie Avenue. Take Leslie Avenue to the end and turn left on British Landing Road. Go past the end of the airport and turn right on Annex Road. Then turn right on Stonecliffe Road (marked). Check out Stonecliffe and then take Stonecliffe Road back to the Annex Road and turn right. Follow Annex Road past the cottages on your right and to the Carriage Tour barns. Turn right and go straight down Cadotte Avenue, past the Grand Hotel (use your brakes!). Turn left on Market Street, then right on Fort Street back to Marquette Park.

FREIGHTER WATCHING

Freighter watching is an art form on Mackinac Island. Summer residents track the comings and goings and pride themselves on being able to name the freighters without looking through binoculars.

A quick primer: boats headed west are usually "down bound and full" of iron ore from the Minnesota area. They've passed through Lake Superior, the Sault Ste. Marie boat locks (Soo), and upper Lake Huron, and are headed for Lake Michigan, Chicago, and Gary, Indiana. They usually return empty in three or four days. The largest freighters on the Great Lakes are 1,000 feet. Occasionally, you see a "salty," or ocean-going vessel, distinguished by its short length and tall superstructure.

FISHING

The Straits are an excellent location to catch king, coho, and kokanee salmon, brown and lake trout, and steelheads. Because the water is so shallow near the shore and there is so much activity in the harbor, fishing off the shore or the boat docks is not recommended. There are several charter companies that will take you out for a half- or full-day adventure, and will provide all the equipment. Rates average $200 for four people for a half-day, and $300 for a full day. Michigan fishing licenses are extra, and are usually available from the charter companies.   To arrange a charter, contact one of the following:

East Bay Charters, Captain Larry Waldecker, 906/643-8051

Mackinac Island Charters, Captain Ross Naeve, 517/733-8585

Northern Lakes Charters, Captain Mike Pounovich, 616/436-5418

Straits Charter, Captain Mark Hendges, 906/643-8310.

Woodsmoke Charters, Captain John Shuler, 906/643-8835.

GOLF

There are two nine-hole golf courses on the island.   The Jewel is located at the Grand Hotel and features beautiful landscaping and views of the Straits.   Greens fees for nine holes at the Jewel are $18 for non-guests and $12 for Grand Hotel guests.   Electric carts are $10 and pull carts are $2.50. Club rental is $5.   There is a small pro shop on the golf course.   Call 847-3331 to arrange a tee time.

The Wawashkmo Golf Links is a favorite with island regulars, and is located in the middle of the island on a portion of an 1814 battlefield.   It is one of the few traditional Scottish links courses in the United States, for the golfer who is ready to tackle the rough.   Greens fees at Wawashkmo are $12 for nine holes or $16 for all day. Electric carts are $10, pull carts are $1, and club rental is $4.   Call 847-3871 to arrange a tee time.

A third golf course is under construction as this book is being written.   Look for Stonecliffe to have a nine-hole golf course near the airport by 1990.

HIKING

The possibilities for a wonderful hike are endless.   Consult the map on page 14 or try one of my favorites:

Woodsy Walk -- approximately 1 1/2 - 2 hours, on a mix of trails and roads. Natural and historic sights. Walk to the back of Marquette Park behind the Indian Dormitory and find Crow's Nest Trail (behind the playground). Follow this up the hill. Turn right on Huron Road and follow past the East Bluff cottages and the beautiful views of the harbor. When you reach Mission Hill (marked "bicycles caution"), stay to the left and continue past more cottages. Watch for Winnebago Trail on your left (it is marked). Take Winnebago to the end.

Go across the paved road, and pick up Rock Trail, a small path that goes to the left. Turn right from Rock Trail onto Lime Kiln Trail. Take Lime Kiln until it ends at the North Bicycle Trail (blacktop) and turn right. Go a short distance and turn left on Rifle Range Road (paved). Watch for a stairway on your right, and take it up to Fort Holmes. After exploring Fort Holmes, follow Fort Holmes Road (the sign says Point Lookout), past the water station, and bear right. Look at the view of Sugar Loaf from Point Lookout, then continue down the hill and turn left on Garrison Road.

At the intersection of three roads, stay to the left and pass the cemeteries. At Skull Cave, bear right. At another intersection of three roads, turn right on Huron Road. Pass Fort Mackinac. At the Governor's summer residence, turn left and take Fort Street down the hill to Marquette Park.

Eastern Experience -- approximately 3 - 4 hours, winding around the island's eastern bluff. Some trails challenging; not recommended for small children. From Marquette Park, take Main Street east (away from town). Turn left on the first road (Bogan Lane, which is just past Inn on Mackinac). Take the stairs at the end of Bogan Lane up the bluff and turn right. Go past the East Bluff cottages and at the first intersection take the high road (sign says Arch Rock). Pass more cottages. Pick up Manitou Trail on your right near where the fence stops on your right (it is marked). Follow Manitou along the bluff until you reach Arch Rock. Check out Arch Rock and then take the

**There are over 50 marked trails
through the island's interior.**

stairway up to the Nicolet Watch Tower.   Pick up Tranquil
Bluff Trail and follow it along the bluff.

When you reach the small green electric company box
marked "caution," pick up Leslie Avenue (paved road to
your left) and continue in the same direction as before,
paralleling the bluff.   Turn left on Murray Trail (marked

with a brown post). Take Murray Trail to Crooked Tree Road (gravel) and turn left. Follow Crooked Tree Road past the North Bicycle Trail (blacktop) and to its end. Turn right on Sugar Loaf Road (gravel) and follow it around Sugar Loaf and to the first intersection. Turn right onto Rifle Range Road and follow it a short distance.

Go up the stairway on your right to Fort Holmes. Explore Fort Holmes, then take the main road (Fort Holmes Road) to Morning Snack Trail and turn right. This is an excellent area to see spring wild flowers. Turn left on Beechwood Trail, follow it to the end, and then go left on Garrison Road. Go past the cemeteries, staying left at the paved intersection. Pass Skull Cave, and then bear right. Bear right again at the main intersection and go past the back of Fort Mackinac. Turn left at the Governor's summer residence, and take Fort Street back down to Marquette Park.

HORSEBACK RIDING

Many who know the island well claim the best way to experience it is from the back of a horse. Few places are so geared to horseback riders.

Rental horses are available from three stables: Cindy's (847-3572) on Market Street between Astor and Hoban, Chambers' (847-6231) at the corner of Market and Cadotte, and Jack's (847-3391) on Mahoney Avenue between Cadotte and Lake Shore Drive. All horses are rented with western tack, and guides are generally provided. It's best to go early in the day, when the horses are fresh. Hourly fees are $15 per person for the first hour and $12 for each hour thereafter. Plan to take at least two hours for a worthwhile trek. Unless you want saddle sores as a souvenir, don't wear shorts while riding. On most days, it's a good idea to take a sweat shirt, because the woods are cooler than Main Street.

Saddle horses are not permitted on Main Street, Huron Street, Lake Shore Drive, Turkey Hill, or in front of the

Grand Hotel.   All of the rental companies will escort you up the Grand Hill, so you should plan your route accordingly. From there, the summer homes at the Annex, Allouez Trail, and Fort Holmes are all pleasant destinations.   If you have more time available, you may want to explore Leslie Avenue, Crooked Tree Road, or the Soldier's Garden.

For those who want to work their horses in a ring-like environment, Turtle Park is the best bet.   It's located near the cemeteries (see map on page 14) and is a project of the Mackinac Island Recreation Association.   Other flat locations to work a horse include the inside of Fort Holmes and the Soldier's Garden.

Let your horses walk back to the barn so they arrive cooled down and ready for their next trip.

The best way to see the island's trails is from the back of a horse.

JOGGING

With over 140 miles of road and trails on the island, the number of different jogging routes is endless. Use the map on page 14 to design your route, or choose one of my favorites:

'Round the Rock -- One lap around the perimeter of the island is 8.2 miles of level, paved ground with the constant opportunity to cool off in the lake. Morning or early evening is best for this route, so you don't have as much bicycle traffic to fight.

Arch Rock Climb -- is about three miles and includes a trip past Arch Rock and the East Bluff cottages, stairs, and a steep downhill. Beginning at Marquette Park, run east along Main Street, past Mission Point Resort, and to the Arch Rock stairway. Run up the stairs to Arch Rock (last time I counted it was 177 stairs), pick up Arch Rock Road (with your back to Arch Rock, it's the main paved road on your left). Take Arch Rock Road to Huron Road (major intersection) and turn left. Follow Huron in front of the East Bluff cottages, turn right at Mission Hill, and at the bottom of the hill, turn right on Main Street to return to Marquette Park.

SAILING

The Straits area is a wonderful place to sail, and a stroll past the marina will whet your appetite. If you have your own sailboat, enjoy it (see Chapter Three for marina information). Unfortunately, there isn't currently a sailboat rental or charter service on the island. Anyone looking for a business opportunity?

SCUBA DIVING

The Department of Natural Resources has named portions of the Straits area a bottomlands preserve, protecting it from alteration. There are a number of shipwrecks in the area, including the Cedarville, a 588-foot self-unloader built in 1927, whose hull is in 35 feet of water, and the schooner M. Stalker, built in 1863, in 80 feet of water. Contact the Straits Scuba Center for information: (906) 643-7001 or (517) 356-9336, or write Thunder Bay Divers, 1105 Partridge Point Marina, Alpena, MI 49707.

STONE SKIPPING

Stone skipping is a serious sport on Mackinac Island. Every July 4th, masters and amateurs gather at Windermere Point for a tense showdown to determine who will be the year's International Stone Skipping and Gerplunking Champion. The current record is 29 skips. If you want to enter, you should be aware that non-island rocks must be sterilized to ensure they do not "pollute" the Straits. Rumor is that the hard-core skippers go to Round Island to get the smoothest stones!

You can practice stone skipping anywhere, but the water is usually calmest between British Landing and Mission Point. Watch out for the swimmers!

Rainy Days

It won't rain during your Mackinac Island excursion, honest. But supposing it did, here are 10 things you could do on the island on a rainy day:

Take a carriage tour. The horses don't mind getting wet, and you'll stay dry while seeing the sights.

Spend the day at the Grand Hotel. Pay your $5 admission fee, and then enjoy. It's the best spot for indoor shopping, a great place to people watch, and you'll feel luxurious!

Sit on the front porch of a hotel, sip hot coffee or cocoa, and listen to the sound of the foghorn.

Explore the Indian Dormitory. Rainy days are the best days to learn about the island's history, because you don't feel compelled to be out enjoying the sunshine.

Go the the library. It has an excellent selection for a small town library, and the librarian can fill you in on the local gossip.

Go fishing. My dad always told me that fishing is better in the rain. (See page 125.)

Go to Mission Point Resort. If you're lucky, there will be a fire in one of the five fireplaces in the lobby. They have a library area with a selection of popular books, and comfortable public areas for relaxing.

Go shopping downtown. You can dart between awnings and stay fairly dry. Because there are fewer people on the island when it rains, the shops are less crowded. Have a contest and see who can find the tackiest souvenir!

Explore Fort Mackinac and the historic buildings on Market Street.

Go to Alford's drug store and buy a game. This is a perfect time to brush up on your gin rummy, Monopoly, or Clue skills.

And take heart. Island insiders love rainy days. There are fewer people and the pace is even slower than usual.

SWIMMING

The following hotels have swimming pools for their guests' use: Chippewa, Grand, Lake View (indoors), Mission Point Resort, and Stonecliffe. The Grand Hotel makes its serpentine pool and surrounding grounds available to non-guests for a daily per person charge of $6. To really pamper yourself on a warm summer day, go the the Grand pool when it opens at 10 a.m., and stay all day. Beverage and food service is available, as are a sauna and whirlpool.

The sparkling waters of Lake Huron and the Straits of Mackinac are extremely inviting if the weather is warm and you like cold water. Water temperatures average 50 degrees in June and warm to about 70 degrees by August. Favorite "swimming holes" include the end of the boardwalk on the west end of town, the British Landing area, the Arch Rock area, and the cove at Mission Point. You should wear sneakers or rubber flip-flops (they float) into the water unless your feet are tough and can handle the rocky bottom. The water generally gets deep very gradually and undertow is not much of a problem (except at Mission Point, where the drop-off is rapid, and the freighters moving through the Straits can cause strange currents in the cove). Swimming near the boat docks or off Windermere Point is dangerous and not recommended.

For sunbathers, Mission Point is probably the most comfortable, as you can settle down on the lawn and still be near the water. In all the other locations, you will have to contend with the island's limestone heritage. If you'd rather watch people than freighters while you get bronze, Marquette Park is a favorite.

TENNIS

There are four sets of tennis courts on the island: Fort Mackinac, Grand Hotel, Mission Point Resort, and Stonecliffe. None of the courts have lights.

My favorites are the ones near Fort Mackinac, just north of the Fort off the South Bicycle Trail. There are three courts in the woods, blocked from the wind, and free to the public.

The Grand has four excellent clay courts that are available for $15 per court per hour for non-guests and $10 per court hour for Grand Hotel guests. Racquets are available for $2. Call the hotel at 847-3331 to reserve a court time.

Mission Point Resort has three courts that are free for its guests and $5 per person per hour for non-guests. Racquets are available for $2 for guests and $3 for non-guests. On a calm day, the courts are fine, but check the courts out before trying to play on a windy day. Call 847-3312 to arrange a court time.

Stonecliffe has two courts that are free to its guests.

VITA COURSE

The Grand Hotel has a half-mile vita course near its tennis and swimming area. It combines a jogging trail (wood chip base) and exercise stations. Although it is designed for guests' use, if it isn't too crowded (and it usually isn't) the public is permitted to use the course. The first station is by the Grand tennis shop.

WEIGHT LIFTING

Mission Point Resort is the only hotel that has a weight room for its guests' use. It features free weights, weight machines, and exercise bicycles, and is free for hotel guests. They are considering opening to the public for a fee. (Call 847-3312 to find out what they decided!) Mackinac Island Recreation and Development has a small weight room in the Community House on Market Street that is sometimes available to the public for a nominal fee. Call 847-6293 to find out fees and times.

11
GETTING ATTACHED

It happens; people fall in love with this island called Mackinac. College students come up for a summer and never leave. Visitors return year after year. Couples get married on the island. People wait for their dream house to come up for sale.

If you feel the fever, read on. I'll describe many ways to have a more "intimate" relationship with the island.

ROMANTIC ENCOUNTERS

For a romantic outing, try one of the following:

Call one of the private carriage tour companies (see Chapter Six) and arrange a *moonlight tour*.

Take a *picnic to Sunset Rock* and watch the sun set. Sunset Rock is high on the west bluff of the island, near Stonecliffe. Consult the map on page 14. From Stonecliffe, go behind the Mansion and across the back lawn. Pick up the trail on the far left back corner of the lawn, follow it to the right, and you'll find Sunset Rock.

Go to *Fort Holmes to watch the stars.* See the map on page 14 to find your way. Fort Holmes is the highest point on the island, and on a clear night, the stars are spectacular.

Stroll along the boardwalk. Sit and listen to the waves lapping against the shore. It's extra special on foggy nights, when you can hear the eerie sound of the foghorn and the pleasant chug-chug of a freighter going by.

Take a picnic to Brown's Brook. On the western side of the island, Brown's Brook is an easy bike ride from downtown, and if you follow it up away from the Lake Shore Road, the brook is a world away from the crowds.

Get married! Mackinac Island's popularity as a place to get married has increased dramatically in recent years. In 1988, there were about 500 weddings on the island, with 14 on one day (August 8, 1988). Carriage Tours has added a full-time wedding consultant to help couples plan their events. (Contact Mackinac Island Wedding Services at 906/847-3573.) All the churches make their facilities available for weddings and a number of the hotels have appropriate banquet facilities. Florists, bakeries, photographers, and musicians are all available.

SUMMER JOBS

Summer employees make the island work. About 3,500 of them come every year, seeking a combination of relaxation, good times, and money. The good times and the relaxation are almost guaranteed, as is hard work. The money depends on the job and the individual. The bulk of the workers are college-age. Most of the jobs are in restaurants, hotels, and shops. Wages are typically minimum, except for tipping positions, which pay less than minimum. Housing is the biggest hassle and expense. Employers generally provide housing and deduct the cost from the employee's paycheck.

St. Anne's church is one of the four churches available for summer weddings on the island.

Workers usually work six long days a week during the peak season. Some don't make it past July 4th, when they realize the work is hard, and it's a long way from home. Others come back year after year, enjoying the camaraderie and the locale. Businesses have a difficult time keeping the workers until the end of the season, so many are offering bonuses to those who stay.

If you are interested in a summer job, contact the Chamber of Commerce for more information (906/847-3787 or P.O. Box 451, Mackinac Island, MI 49757). They will provide you with a list of employers, and a brochure describing what to expect. It's best to inquire in the fall or winter.

LONGER STAYS

There are many options for those who would enjoy a longer stay on the island. As indicated in Chapter Four, Pontiac Lodge, Stonecliffe, and Silver Birches have reasonably priced weekly rates.

If you are interested in staying in one of the historic cottages, be aware that home owners whose homes are on state land cannot rent their homes out for less than two weeks, or to more than one family at a time. Rentals range from about $2,000 to $4,000 for two weeks. These regulations generally apply to homes downtown and on the East and West Bluffs. The homes in the Annex and the Stonecliffe development are on private property, so the state regulations do not apply. Contact Mackinac Island Properties (906/847-3355), the island's only full-time real estate agency, or look in the island newspaper, the *Town Crier* for advertisements. Sometimes the Chamber of Commerce has a list of available rentals (see address above). It's best to make arrangements one year in advance, but occasionally, homes are available at the last minute.

If you are really hooked, check out the real estate market. Historically, there have been very few homes available, as the older homes tend to be "kept in the family" and the state owns 80% of the island land that could be considered for new construction. But in the early 1980's the real estate market on the island changed dramatically when Stonecliffe began developing some of its 175 acres of private land. Home sites are available in the $25,000 -

$50,000 range and condominiums are available in the
$93,500 - $150,000 range.   Restrictions on this property
require the building plans to be Victorian in style and
approved in advance.   The market for the older, historic
homes is still very tight.   Approximately seven have
changed hands in the past three years, and prices have
ranged from about $200,000 to $675,000.   Contact Mackinac
Island Properties (906/847-3355) or watch the *Town Crier*
if you are interested.

**Home prices have escalated some since this house
was built in 1885 for $2,000.**

CONVENTIONS AND GROUP TRAVEL

If you want to bring your business associates to the island,
or plan a class reunion or the like, do it.   The island's
relaxing atmosphere provides a great backdrop for
business or social outings.   The Grand Hotel, Mission Point
Resort, and the Lake View Hotel are the primary
convention hotels, with ample meeting space and experts
on hand to help you with your planning.   A number of the
other hotels also have one or two meeting rooms available

if your group is small. All the hotels have group rates available. If you want help planning your convention or group outing, contact Mackinac Connection, Inc. (906/847-3496 - summer, 313/542-4194 - winter). They can help you select a hotel, plan meal functions, transportation, and special events.

STAYING IN TOUCH

The best way to stay in touch with the action on Mackinac Island is to subscribe to the island newspaper, the *Town Crier* (906/847-3788). The *Town Crier* is published weekly during the season, and has one issue in the winter. Subscriptions are $8.50, and can be purchased at the *Town Crier* offices on Market Street or by writing to: P.O. Box 532, Mackinac Island, MI 49757. Individual issues can be purchased for $.35 from paper stands on Main Street and Market Street.

GETTING INVOLVED

There are many ways to get involved with the island activities during or after your stay. See the *Town Crier* for weekly events, and stop in on a few. A number of organizations have been created to funnel money and energy into important island activities. Some of the more active groups are:

Mackinac Associates -- Founded by the Mackinac Island State Park Commission (MISPC), Mackinac Associates acts as a "friends" organization to MISPC. It is funded through memberships and contributions, and takes on projects such as the renovation of Mission Church and educational programs for children. Individual memberships are $30 and family memberships are $50. Membership provides unlimited admission to Fort Mackinac, Michilimackinac, and Old Mill Creek and an informative newsletter about historical activities. Membership can be purchased in the Administrative Office of Fort Mackinac, or write to: Box 370, Mackinac Island, MI 49757.

Mackinac Island Recreation and Development (MIRD) -- MIRD's goal is to improve the recreational facilities on the island for year-round residents and summer visitors. They are funded by contributions, the sale of an island calendar (available in most island shops), and a fashion show during the Lilac Festival.   MIRD is responsible for developing Great Turtle Park, a recreational area that includes a softball field, basketball court, playground equipment and an equestrian ring.   Their long-range plans include building an Olympic size pool and community center at Turtle Park.   Call (906/847-6293) or write (P.O. Box 421, Mackinac Island, MI 49757) for more information.

Friends of the Mackinac Island Medical Center -- This organization conducts fund-raisers and seeks contributions to offset the operating expense of the Mackinac Island Medical Center.   Stop in at the Center on Market Street, call (906/847-3583), or write to them (P.O. Box 536, Mackinac Island, MI 49757) for information.

Mackinac Island Humane Society -- A watchdog group interested in improving the treatment of animals on the island, the Humane Society accepts donations to help offset expenses.   Call them on 906/847-3583 or write to: P.O. Box 461, Mackinac Island, MI 49757.

Stella King Scholarship Fund -- Named in honor of the long-time island nurse, the Stella King Scholarship Fund seeks donations to help send island children to college. Write to them at P.O. Box 340, Mackinac Island, MI 49757.

SPECIAL REMINDERS

Shop for a special reminder of your island trip.   My favorites:

A book about the island.   Two all-star gift books are <u>Mackinac Island, Its History In Pictures</u>, by Eugene T.

Petersen, and <u>Mackinac, The Gathering Place</u>, Russell
McKee, editor.

Fudge. Preferably several pounds, in a variety of flavors.
You can buy 12 pounds, put it in the freezer, and take one
pound out a month until your next visit (see page 87).

An island map or calendar. Every year MIRD produces a
great calendar with island photographs. The Chamber of
Commerce and some of the stores sell island maps.

Photograph, print, or painting with an island theme.
There are lots of these available, and they are lasting
reminders of your trip.

Island theme scrimshaw piece. Scrimshaw makes you feel
like you are near the water. If you add to that an island
theme, you have a wonderful Mackinac memento.

Sweatshirt, T-shirt, or hat with Mackinac written
somewhere. With the variety available, it could take you
all day to pick the right one.

Horseshoe. Where the horse is king, what could be a
better remembrance or good luck charm?

Island duffel bag. The Grand shops carry these, and they
are pricey, but very stylish.

Photographs of your group at island landmarks. Try Arch
Rock or Sugar Loaf for some drama.

ACTING LIKE A LOCAL

With a little coaching, it isn't hard for a visitor to pass as a
local. Here are some tongue-in-cheek suggestions, taken
from Hugh McVeigh's "What you always wanted to know
about Mackinac Island but were afraid to ask." Copyright,
Hugh McVeigh, 1975.

Never pronounce the island's name "Mack-i-nack." The "nac" is pronounced "naw." Never spell the island's name Mackinaw, or the city on the mainland's name Mackinac. Mackina<u>c</u> Island and Mackina<u>w</u> City are the correct spellings. The bridge is spelled with a "c."

Take your own bike and buy a Mackinac Island license at the Police Station. This is an obvious badge of "belonging." Riding a rental bike is very fudgie (see page 149). If you have a fold-up bike, there isn't much you can do. You are obviously a boater.

Always buy one-way ferry boat tickets, even though it is more expensive. It will look like you aren't planning on leaving the island. On the ferry, always go to the back of the boat, stretch out and act bored. Never look at the bridge (and don't call it "Big Mac") or at any passing freighters. Never wave at people on passing ferry boats.

Hide your camera and fudge.

The bridge should not be called "Big Mac."

Always ride your licensed bike to the right and give horses the right-of-way.

At night, act unconcerned about the bats even if they terrify you.

Buy a bag of groceries and carry it around all day.

Never look up at the Fort when they shoot the cannon.

Call the Chippewa Hotel the "Chip" and the Village Inn the "V.I."

When calling from the island to another Mackinac Island location, dial only the last four digits of the telephone number.

❝ *They call me the man who fudged his way to success. I like that. When I came to Mackinac Island in the 1950's, the timing was right for an expanding candy business. And fudge was everyone's favorite. It caught on so we put out great big buttons that read, 'I'm a Mackinac Island fudgie,' and the day tourists wore them with pride. That's the way the term fudgie, meaning day tourist, was coined.* ❞

Harry Ryba
Island Business Owner

12
NATIVE KNOWLEDGE

ADDRESSES -- There aren't any street addresses on Mackinac Island. All mail is picked up at the post office by island residents. Directions are given by major landmark.

AIRPORT -- Mackinac Island Airport is a paved, lighted, 3,500 foot airstrip in the center of the island. See Chapter Three for more information, or call them at 906/847-3231.

ARCADE GAMES -- Arcade games (video or pinball) are available at the arcades on Astor Street and in the Orphan Corner Mall (near Shepler Dock), Doud's Grocery Store, the Balsam Shop, the Pilot House, Mission Point Resort, and the Grand Hotel.

BATS -- Spend an evening on Mackinac Island and you'll likely meet a real native, the island bat. They are even more afraid of you than you are of them, so don't be concerned. The bats serve an excellent purpose, keeping the island almost mosquito-free.

BANKING -- There is one bank on the island, the First National Bank of St. Ignace - Mackinac Island branch (906/847-3732). It is on Market Street, between Astor and Hoban. It can handle all your basic needs, including traveler's checks, credit card advances, and wire transfers. There was big excitement on the island in 1989 when an automatic teller machine was added (Cirrus and Network 1 compatible). The bank's hours are 8:30 a.m. - 4:00 p.m. in the summer.

BICYCLE AUCTION -- If you are interested in an unusual shopping experience, attend the Mackinac Island bicycle auction, held at the Police Station on Market Street on the second Saturday in June. Over 200 bicycles that have been impounded or abandoned, or have otherwise fallen into police custody are auctioned, usually at rock-bottom prices.

BICYCLE FLAGS -- Bicycle flags can scare horses. Take yours off or wrap the flag around the pole and secure it.

CAMPING -- Camping is not allowed on Mackinac Island. Mackinaw City and St. Ignace both have campgrounds; contact the Chambers of Commerce for information (see below).

CHAMBER OF COMMERCE -- The Mackinac Island Chamber of Commerce is located on Main Street between Fort and Astor, on the north side. The friendly folks there can answer almost any question you might have about the island. You can reach them year-round by calling (906/847-3783) or writing: P.O. Box 451, Mackinac Island, MI 49757. They have a very useful informational package that they will send you about the island and the Chamber members' businesses.

The Mackinaw City Chamber of Commerce can be reached at 616/436-5574 or P.O. Box 856 Mackinaw City, MI 49710. The St. Ignace Chamber of Commerce can be reached at 906/643-8717 or 11 S. State Street, St. Ignace, MI 49781.

The Mackinac Island Chamber of Commerce is open 9:00 a.m. to 6:00 p.m. daily in the summer.

CHURCHES -- There are three churches on the island: St. Anne's Catholic Church (847-3507), on the corner of Huron Street and Church Street east of town; Trinity Episcopal Church (847-3798) on Fort Street just past Market Street; and the Little Stone Congregational Church (847-3877), on Cadotte Avenue. Check the *Town Crier* for service times.

DRAYS -- Horse-drawn drays are the primary method of moving freight on the island. You can identify drays by the large draft horses pulling them, and the flat-bed trailer type wagons they pull. Drays are used for moving everything from fresh produce to trash to construction equipment to fuel oil. If you need dray service, call the Mackinac Island Service Company at 847-6174.

ELECTRICITY -- Huge underwater cables bring electricity to the island from generators on the mainland operated by the Edison Sault Electric Company.

FIRE -- The island has an all-volunteer fire department and one motorized fire truck. When the alarm sounds, fire fighters drop what they are doing, hop on their bicycles, and race to the Police Station to join the fire truck. The department has done an excellent job of containing fires on the island, quite a feat considering that most of the structures are all wood. The Fire Department phone is 847-3300 for emergencies. If you hear a siren at noon, or a little after, it probably isn't a fire; the fire siren goes off at noon "island time" (see below).

Fires are not allowed on the island without a permit from the Police Department.

FLORISTS -- The island has two florists. Sawyer's Greenhouse (847-3972) is one of the country's oldest greenhouses continually operating from the same location. Sawyer's is open year-round, specializing in geraniums. They handle weddings, holiday wreaths, and planting and maintenance for home owners. Trillium Garden (847-6228) opened in 1989. It offers landscape design, floral arrangements, and maintenance. Trillium also has a fruit and vegetable market. Both greenhouses are in the block behind St. Anne's church.

FUDGIES -- The name given to day tourists by islanders. Fudgies can usually be identified by the cameras around their necks and the pound of fudge in their hands.

GOVERNMENT -- The island has two governing bodies: the City of Mackinac Island and the Mackinac Island State Park Commission. They work together to ensure that the island successfully makes its transition every year from an isolated small town of 600 people in the winter to a major tourism center in the summer.

The City of Mackinac Island is run by a mayor and a city council. It has responsibility for municipal services (water, sewer, and waste), police and fire protection, and maintenance of the city streets, cemeteries, and city-owned buildings. The City generates income through property taxes, business and motor vehicle permits, and fees paid by ferry companies based on a percentage of their revenue.

The Mackinac Island State Park Commission is a commission appointed by the governor that has responsibility for the state park land (80% of the island), including the historic buildings, trails, and roads, the Governor's summer residence, the airport, and land leases. The MISPC has a small year-round staff, and offices at Fort Mackinac and in Lansing, Michigan. The state operations on the island are funded through proceeds from ticket sales at historic buildings, sale of revenue bonds, and state appropriations.

HUNTING -- Hunting is not allowed on Mackinac Island.

ICE BRIDGE -- The waters usually freeze between British Landing or the Stonecliffe area on the island and St. Ignace, providing an "ice bridge" or winter highway for island residents. The bridge usually lasts from January to March, and residents travel it on foot, cross-country skis, or snowmobile (or "snowmachines" as islanders call them).

"ISLAND TIME" -- A term affectionately used by insiders to describe Mackinac's own measurement of time. Often used synonymously with "slow" or "when we get to it." As in, "the taxi will be there at 2:00 p.m. 'island time.'" Opposite of prompt.

Over 800,000 people come
to Mackinac Island every year.

LAUNDRY -- There is a coin-operated laundry available on the second floor of Orphan's Corner Mall, on the west end of town.

LIBRARY -- The library (847-3421) is on Market Street, between Astor and Hoban. Summer hours are weekdays noon to 6:00 p.m., except for Wednesdays when it is open until 8:00 p.m. Cards are inexpensive, and the selection is good for such a small library.

LIGHTHOUSES -- There are two lighthouses visible from Mackinac Island. The Round Island lighthouse was built in 1895 and was used continuously for 52 years. It was replaced in 1947 by the white automatic beacon that can be seen near the break wall.

LILACS -- June is lilac time on Mackinac Island. If you time your trip right, you'll be able to smell the lilacs as you approach the harbor. Most of the lilacs were imported to the island by the French.   Marquette Park has the largest concentration of lilac trees on the island.

LITTER -- Don't do it.   Much of Mackinac Island's attractiveness comes from its natural beauty.   Respect that, and if you take a picnic into the park, bring back your litter.   You shouldn't need extra encouragement, but in case you do, there is a fine for littering on Mackinac Island.   Sorry for the sermon!

**There are over 2,500 bicycles
on the island in the summer.**

LIQUOR -- Doud's grocery store is the only packaged liquor store on the island. See Chapter Six for listing of restaurants that serve liquor. Some of the bars also have beer and wine to go. The drinking age in Michigan is 21. Because of the concentration of young people working on the island, the taverns strictly enforce the drinking age.

LOCKERS -- If you brought more gear than you can carry, small lockers are available near the Star Line dock and at the Shepler dock, on the west end of town.

LOTTERY -- State of Michigan lottery tickets are available at Doud's grocery store.

MACKINAC BRIDGE -- The Mackinac Bridge is a five-mile long suspension bridge that connects Michigan's upper and lower peninsulas at St. Ignace and Mackinaw City. It was completed in 1957, after three years of difficult construction. The continual maintenance is funded through user tolls ($1.50 per car one-way). Each year on Labor Day, Michigan's Governor leads 50,000 or so thrill seekers on a walk over the bridge.

MEDICAL -- The Mackinac Island Medical Center is on Market Street between Fort and Astor. If you need medical attention, call 847-3582 days or 847-3962 evenings and weekends, or stop by. The Center is staffed by a doctor, two residents, a nurse, and an X-ray technician during the summer. The doctors are on rotation from Beaumont Hospital near Detroit.

The Center is equipped to handle most island incidents (bike accidents and the like), but for more serious situations, patients may be transported to the mainland by boat or airplane.

Ambulance service is run by a team of volunteer Emergency Medical Technicians. They do have a motorized ambulance. Call 847-3344.

MOVIES -- For a real island experience, go to a movie on Mackinac Island. It's a big community outing; first-run movies are shown regularly at the Mission Point Resort Theater (847-3312) on Monday nights. Check the *Town Crier* for the week's movie. Sometimes the Grand Hotel (847-3331) has movies available for its guests.

Two movies have been filmed on Mackinac Island. *This Time for Keeps*, starring Esther Williams and Jimmy Durante, was filmed in 1946. *Somewhere In Time*, starring Christopher Reeves and Jane Seymour, was filmed in 1979. The island has a full motion picture sound stage at Mission Point Resort, which was built by Moral Re-Armament to produce MRA promotional films, and is currently used for special events.

NEWSPAPERS -- The island newspaper, the *Town Crier* (847-3788), is published weekly during the summer, and once during the winter. Copies are available at all the newsstands and from the offices on Market Street behind Trafalgar Square.

The *Detroit Free Press, Detroit News, Wall Street Journal*, *USA Today*, and *Chicago Tribune* are available from newsstands located outside Doud's grocery store, near the Star Line dock, near the Arnold Line dock, and across from the Post Office. The Detroit papers and *USA Today* arrive on the first boat (7:45 a.m. in the summer) and the other papers arrive between 10:00 and 11:00 a.m. *The New York Times* is available on a day-late basis from the Grand Hotel Tobacconist Shop, but call ahead (847-3331) to reserve a copy of the Sunday *Times*.

PLAYGROUNDS -- There are three playgrounds on the island: 1) behind the Indian Dormitory; 2) at the island school, past the west end of town; and 3) at Great Turtle Park in the interior of the island (see map on page 14).

PHOTO PROCESSING -- Same-day photo processing is available at the Balsam Shop on Main Street and Mackinac Island Photography at Surrey Hills. Benjamin's on Main Street also handles film processing.

POLICE -- Mackinac has three year-round police officers. About six additional officers and two state troopers join the force for the summer season. The most common crimes are alcohol-related and bicycle theft. The police station has a two-cell jail. The Police Station is located on the corner of Market and Astor Streets. Call 847-3344.

POST OFFICE -- The Post Office (847-3821) is on Market Street, between Fort and Astor. It is open from 8:30 a.m. - 5:30 p.m. on weekdays in the summer, and 9:00 a.m. - 1:00 p.m. on Saturdays. They have express mail service. All of the residents pick up their mail at the post office (from a post office box or "general delivery"), eliminating costly door-to-door delivery, so it is one of the few profitable post offices in the country.

RASPBERRIES -- Delicious wild raspberries grow in many of the island's meadows. Look for them in mid-August. Just past the end of the airport runway is usually a good spot.

An aerial view of downtown Mackinac Island.

REVEILLE -- At 9:00 a.m., be prepared for the uplifting sounds of reveille coming from Fort Mackinac.

REST ROOMS -- Public rest rooms are located: 1) behind the Chamber of Commerce office on Main Street in the middle of downtown; 2) inside the Visitor's Center across from Marquette Park; 3) near the Star Line Dock on the west end of town; 4) at Arch Rock; and 5) inside the British Landing Nature Center.

ROCK -- A not-so-affectionate term used for Mackinac Island by insiders who need a dose of the mainland. As in, "I need to get off this rock."

ROLLER-SKATING -- Roller-skating is not allowed on the island, because it frightens some horses.

SCHOOL -- The island has one public school, housing kindergarten through 12th grade. There are usually about 90 students and ten teachers. The 1989 graduating class was six students. It has boys' and girls' basketball and volleyball teams that play in the Northern Lights League under the name "Lakers". The league is the smallest in the state, with a combined high school enrollment of 90 students.

SCOUTS -- The Mackinac Island State Park Commission conducts a program to bring scouting troops to the island for a week of recreation and assistance to the MISPC. A different Michigan troop comes to the island each week in the summer, stays in the barracks near Fort Mackinac, and assists at state properties such as the Fort, the Indian Dormitory, and the Beaumont Memorial. Interested troop leaders should contact the commission (P.O. Box 370, Mackinac Island, MI 49757) the summer before they are interested in participating in the program.

SEAPLANE TOURS -- Seaplane tours of the Straits area are available from Huron Air Service. Stop by and see them at the Star Line Dock in St. Ignace or call them (906/643-7774) to make arrangements. Rates are $20 - $25 per person and the flight lasts 15 - 20 minutes. They accept Visa and Master Card.

SIZE -- Mackinac Island is about 2,200 acres and is 8.2 miles around and about 3 miles long (from Marquette Park to British Landing).

SKATEBOARDS -- Skateboards are not allowed on Mackinac Island because they are difficult to control and can scare horses.

STREET SWEEPERS -- Street sweepers provide an invaluable service for Mackinac Island, keeping the streets clear of horse residue. They are employed by the city, the Mackinac Island State Park Commission, the Grand Hotel, and each of the carriage tour and horse rental companies.

STROLLERS -- Strollers can be rented from Ryba's (847-6261) or Orr Kids' (847-3211) Bicycle Rentals.

TAPS -- Played at 10:00 p.m. daily at Fort Mackinac.

TAXI -- A horse-drawn carriage dispatched by radio control. Call 847-3323 for service. See Chapter Six for more information.

TELEPHONES -- Pay telephones are located in most of the hotels and in the following locations: marina, Chamber of Commerce, Arnold Line dock, Star Line dock, Taxi Office, Shepler dock, Michigan Bell offices (Hoban Street), Grand Hotel golf course, airport, and British Landing. All phone numbers on the island are area code 906, followed by 847- and then the unique four digit number. You can dial just the last four numbers when calling from any phone on the island. Because the exchange is a rotary exchange, you cannot retrieve messages from an answering machine that requires a push button. And it's just as well!

TRASH -- Because of its limited land availability for trash disposal, the island has had an active trash management system since 1980. All businesses and residents are required to sort their trash into biodegradable and non-biodegradable wastes.   Biodegradable wastes are put into a compost to be used as fertilizer.   Non-biodegradable wastes are buried in a landfill in the island's interior.

WATER -- The island uses Lake Huron as its water source. Water is treated at a plant just east of Mission Point and then stored near Fort Holmes.   Waste water is treated at a plant near the airport.

WHEELCHAIRS -- Wheelchair rentals are available from Alford's Drug Store (847-3881) and Orr Kids' Bicycle Rental (847-3211).

VIDEO RENTAL -- Doud's grocery store (847-3551) has a collection of 200 videos available for rental.   VCR rental is also available.

**Mackinac Island is a great
family vacation destination.**

"_To choose only one best Mackinac memory is nearly impossible, because the island has meant so much to me. There's the excitement of working and playing on the island as a young boy scout. There's the awe of seeing the magnificent Straits of Mackinac for the first time from the Governor's Summer Residence; the thrill of the holes in one on the Grand Hotel's golf course; the pride of hosting many of the 1988 presidential candidates and all of the Midwest governors; the serenity of quiet walks along the many trails; and so many more._

Just as important as the memories is the commitment I share with millions of our citizens to protect and preserve this Michigan jewel so that future generations have the same opportunity to enjoy and treasure Mackinac Island.**"**

Jim Blanchard
Governor
State of Michigan

ADDITIONAL READINGS

For those who are interested in additional readings about Mackinac Island, there are numerous publications. Many of them served as useful sources for this book.

Armour, David and Keith Widder, *At the Crossroads -- Michilimackinac During the American Revolution,* Mackinac Island State Park Commission, Mackinac Island, Mich., 1978.

Fuller, Iola, *The Loon Feather,* Harcourt Brace Jovanavich, Orlando, Fla., 1968.

Gringhuis, Dirk, *Lore of the Great Turtle: Indian Legends of Mackinac Retold,* Mackinac Island State Park Commission, Mackinac Island, Mich., 1970.

McCabe, John, *Grand Hotel: Mackinac Island,* The Unicorn Press, Lake Superior State College, Sault Ste. Marie, Mich., 1987.

McKee, Russell, editor, *Mackinac: The Gathering Place,* Michigan Natural Resources Magazine publication, Lansing, Mich., 1981

Petersen, Eugene, *Mackinac Island: Its History in Pictures,* Mackinac Island State Park Commission, Mackinac Island, Mich., 1973.

Piljac, Pamela and Thomas, *Mackinac Island: Historic Frontier, Timeless Wonderland, Vacation Resort,* Bryce-Waterton Publications, Portage, Ind., 1988.

Porter, Phil and Victor Nelhiebel, *The Wonder of Mackinac,* Mackinac Island State Park Commission, Mackinac Island, Mich., 1984.

Porter, Phil, *View from the Veranda, The History and Architecture of the Summer Cottages on Mackinac Island,* Mackinac Island State Park Commission, Mackinac Island, Mich., 1981.

Rubin, Lawrence, *Mighty Mac -- The Official Picture History of the Mackinac Bridge,* Kiwanis Club of St. Ignace, St. Ignace, Mich., 1958.

Williams, Meade, *Early Mackinac,* Avery Color Studios, Au Train, Mich., 1987 reprint of an 1897 publication.

Widder, Keith, *Dr. Beaumont: The Mackinac Years,* Mackinac Island State Park Commission, Mackinac Island, Mich., 1975.

Wood, Edwin, *Historic Mackinac,* The Macmillan Company, New York, New York, 1918.

WHO IS AMY MCVEIGH, ANYWAY?

Besides being the author of this book, I'm a long-time summer resident of Mackinac Island. I started exploring the island on my Shetland pony when I was six. Since then, I've ridden, hiked, biked, jogged, swam, and skied my way to every corner.

Members of my family have had all sorts of jobs here, including cocktail waitress, fudge flipper, public relations, musician, dock porter, and hotel sales. And we've entertained countless friends and business associates at our island home, Brigadoon. With all the knowledge and love for the island that we have, one of us was destined to write a guidebook. I've always been the organized one in the family, so it's my name on the cover!

My mother and I also own Mackinac Connection, Inc., an independent meeting planning firm specializing in Mackinac Island functions. Before my recent Mackinac business ventures, I spent six years at General Motors, most recently as a marketing manager for its Saturn Corporation subsidiary.

When I'm not on the island, I live in Huntington Woods, Michigan, with my husband Jeff Braun. Besides being an ace photographer and a publishing mogul, Jeff is an attorney.

For those who like academic credentials, I have an undergraduate degree from Boston University's School of Public Communication and an M.B.A. from the Graduate School of Business at Harvard University. But my most important credential is a deep love for Mackinac Island.

I hope you've enjoyed Mackinac Connection: An Insider's Guide. I'd like to hear your comments and suggestions anytime; just write to: Mackinac Publishing, P.O. Box 215, Mackinac Island, Michigan 49757.

HOW TO ORDER MORE COPIES OF
<u>MACKINAC CONNECTION</u>

I hope you loved this book, and want to give copies to all your friends and family.

Additional copies of <u>Mackinac Connection: An Insider's Guide</u> are available from the publisher. Send a check or money order for $8.95 (Michigan residents add 4% sales tax), plus $1.50 for shipping and handling, for each book to:

> Mackinac Publishing
> P.O. Box 215
> Mackinac Island, MI 49757

Please send the check and a letter indicating your full name, address (street, P.O. Box, apartment number, city, state, and zip code), and phone number for shipping. We'll try to get them to you as soon as possible, but please leave two to four weeks, just in case.

I know the island is gaining international popularity, but because we don't have a foreign exchange bank here, please send U.S. funds only.

Thanks!